THE ART OF BEING AN ENTREPRENEURIAL WOMAN

by Zella Jackson

NOVASEARCH PUBLISHING DIVISION
Coarsegold, California

Published By:
Novasearch Publishing
29643 Horseshoe Drive
Coarsegold, CA 93614
(209) 642-6181

Printed in the United States of America
Cover Design by Larry Underhill
Edited by Larry Undrhill

ISBN: 0-9659560-0-8

Turn to the back of this book for information about ordering additional copies.

Acknowledgments

I wish to thank all of the women who have bared their souls to me. It is has been our collective struggle to balance home and work which has inspired this book. In addition, I would like to thank all the men in my life who have shared with me their concerns for their children and wives when the "real" world demanded ever too much.

In particular, I wish to thank my life-long friend, Linda Ferguson, who has managed to find her way as an intrapreneur and single parent of a severely handicapped son; entrepreneur Nancy Hanson who finished her own book in record time and has provided endless encouragement, and Betsy, Dan, and baby Katherine Allen, who have been an inspiration as a model family that has successfully chosen a non-traditional pattern of success.

And how can one adequately thank someone who has been instrumental in giving the gift of life itself? Thank you, Dr. Philip MacNamee for all of your support and encouragement.

I also wish to thank my "guardian angel", Dr. James Dimarchi for his support during a particularly challenging time for me when I almost lost hope for my baby twins. He also "bent the rules" so I could have my trusty computer in the hospital room to begin writing this manuscript.

In addition, I wish to thank Randall Preiser who has always been there for me when I needed a friend. His male perspective has proven invaluable.

Thank you "Auntie" Suni Reedy and "Auntie" Irene Green for your love and attention not only for me but for my children, as well. May God bless all the "godmothers" of the world. You make life so much richer for us all and make meaningful the phrase "it takes a village to raise a child."

Many thanks to my twin Uncles Frank and Donald who took my siblings and me "out of the storm" enough so that one day I might dream a New World.

I also wish to thank my husband's family who have "adopted" me as one of their own: Uncle George, Auntie "Dubby", Auntie Norma, Uncle Bruce, Aunt Debbie, cousins Jeremy, Jacob, and Ethan. In particular, I wish to thank my in-laws who have been like "second parents" to me as well as the best grandparents in the world to my three children.

Finally, I wish to thank my husband of twenty years who has been my most ardent supporter for our vision of a balanced life together through Entrepreneurism. Last but not least, I must thank our eleven-year-old son, Larry, and our two-year-old twins, James and Daisy, for simply being the gifts from God we know them to be and for providing me the wisdom to stop and listen to the true rhythms of womanhood.

Zella Jackson

TABLE OF_CONTENTS

The Art of being an Entrepreneurial Woman

Adopt the new philosophical paradigm for today's successful woman and create *independence, wealth, and power.*

INDEPENDENCE: Self-governing; not looking to others for one's opinions or for guidance in conduct.

WEALTH: Abundance of valuable material possessions or resources.

POWER: Possession of control, authority, or influence over self and others.

Discover Entrepreneurism and resonate with the true rhythms of womanhood.

"IT IS ESSENTIAL THAT ONE UNDERSTANDS ALL SITUATIONS AND CONDITIONS OF LIFE ARE MAN (WOMAN) MADE

... AND

HOW WE THINK DETERMINES OUR LIFE-STYLE, OUR CONDITIONS, AND OUR SELF-IDENTITY."

Eva Weir
Pocketbook of Change

Chapter I

Women In Bondage

Like the pampered kitten
she sits in her contented corner;
Screaming inwardly of pain borne by her.
I seek to warn her.
But it is late and she must get back to sleep
and keep the peace;
keep her place.

As the ultimate fear of loneliness supersedes all
wants and needs; even the need to breathe a breath
of free air...
I care,
even if you can't
anymore.
But, you can -- just try
don't cry.
Weep tears of joy as you seek your freedom...
You are such a gentle revolutionary,
he must love you.

Z.J. 1973

Women In Bondage

Countless women are in bondage in America today. While the shackles are invisible and the smiles of the inmates belie their condition, millions of American women are in bondage just the same. They are trapped in unhappy marriages, childless singledom, dead-end jobs, abusive relationships, financially strapped households living from pay-check to pay-check, and two career families that could other wise be healthy but suffer from too little time to enjoy life.

These women are going to the bookstores in droves to get the latest self-help books on developing a healthy relationship with their partners and children, but most fail to squeeze the necessary time out of a day to devote even a shared meal with loved ones. Millions of women are suffering in abusive relationships whereby the lack of life mastery skills keeps them imprisoned. In addition, many working women can still be found in what the business magazines have dubbed the "pink collar ghettos" -- librarians, teachers, clerks, secretaries with little hope of significant pay raises or promotions. Further, since 1975, 95% of all new welfare recipients have been women with dependent children which strikingly illustrates their desperate need to find a way to become enterprising citizens without sacrificing time with their children.

And yet "staying in" has its pitfalls. The Bureau of Labor Statistics reported in 1993, while 41% of all managers are women, they earn from two thirds to one half their male counterparts. In addition, Working Woman Magazine sports a feature article in its April, 1994 issue entitled, "When You've Been Passed Over", reflecting another common problem for women. Lastly, a 1994 nationwide survey conducted by Wisconsin Survey Research Laboratory revealed while 45% of supervisors are women, only 18% of top executives are female. It would appear the glass ceiling is alive and well in corporate America which leaves millions of women every day wondering how they can make their professional lives work better.

But the time for change is now. And the fact that you picked up this book tells me you are disturbed by these sad statistics, are at least considering making major changes and wish to create for yourself a self-sufficient life. I applaud your actions in taking what may very well be your first steps toward taking charge of your life.

And yet, just starting and running a business is not the complete solution. Women endure a 20% drop in income upon becoming entrepreneurs while their male counterparts, in contrast, increase their income. As a consequence, female entrepreneurs earn a shocking 50% less than their male counterparts. The complete solution must involve strengthening women entrepreneurs' sense of professional worth, vision, self-esteem, and sense of purpose.

But how many women in this coming decade can realistically aspire to become top executives? Likewise, how many women can hope to start and run multi-billion or even multi-million dollar enterprises? What about the millions of women who have a talent and can simply earn a good living and gain the inspiring benefit of never having to worry about being passed up again? How can the woman who undervalues her work and thereby undercharges change her sense of self so that collectively female entrepreneurs stop working at half pay? What of the millions of women who suffer from low self-esteem that need to know self-sufficiency and life mastery skills are the cornerstones of healing? Finally, how can women restructure their lives to earn what they are worth, have ample time for their families, while being self-sufficient and achieving financial independence? These are some of the important questions enterprising women hope to answer for themselves. Herein lies my sense of it.... may you each find your own way.

Many of you may feel the obstacles in your path make it hopeless for you to dream about a life whereby <u>you</u> are in control. Some of you may feel the obstacles are surmountable but you only need guidance on how to best steer your courses. Still others, may simply need a little nudge, some inspiration, and a game plan to get in gear. Whichever category you find yourself in, rest assured you are not alone in your struggle. Trust your instincts when I share with you that the world of enterprising women revolves around overcoming both self-imposed and culturally imposed limitations. The goal is to be aware of what the true obstacles are and maneuver around them. In so doing, you will find independence, wealth, and power.

In September, 1969, I viewed my own life with hopelessness and despair. I recorded these sentiments in my diary saying simply, "Someone threw the key away, the door wouldn't open. Love was the key. The door was me."

You see, I was the child of two poverty-stricken alcoholics who were verbally abusive. I was raised in a neighborhood where crime, multi-generational welfare dependency, teen-age pregnancies, alcohol and drug addictions, high school dropouts, and functional illiteracy were an accepted part of life. In addition, while my family had over two hundred years of miscegenation, the census taker classified us simply as Negroes. And oh, I almost forgot.. I was born female. Sizing up these unfortunate beginnings, my husband once remarked that if I had been hit by a truck in my youth and rendered disabled, I would have met no less than every criteria for disenfranchised people in this country.

While I recognized the low expectations and the negative stereotypes of my "station in life", once I attained adulthood, I managed to have a full, prosperous life free from alcohol, drugs, crime, welfare, and ***even the common dependency most people have on a job***. Along the way, I discovered many "secrets" that literally set me soaring above the quagmire below. One of my most significant lessons was discovering the importance of helping others to expand their own horizons. This process of helping others provided one important mechanism that helped set myself free. Somewhere along the way, I stopped trying to fix myself and began helping others. As it turns out I was able to incorporate this "helping" in the form of both volunteer work as well as in my independent professional life. In both instances I found myself talking primarily to women and women of color and sharing with them the importance of mastering ones life by pursuing entrepreneur ship. I helped women to discover independence through business which in turn, meant gaining independence in life.

These changes will not be easy but they are necessary. Women and especially women of color in America today are standing at the crossroads of a remarkable new era. This new era, unlike previous times is providing institutionalized support vs. institutionalized barriers. As we embark into the next century, women-owned businesses are politically and ethically encouraged. We owe it to our foremothers and, most of all, we owe it to our children to create a better way of life. A life that has time for, well...... enjoying life.

I dedicate this book to all of you, who have looked in the mirror and chosen to see something other than what the media and stereotypes dictate. I applaud you for throwing out all the low expectations of relatives, teachers, employers, and the whole rest of the world. I am inspired and uplifted by those of you who shall manage, against all odds, to grow into the best human being you were destined to become. Here are the "secrets" that have guided me. Add them to your own insights and the rest of the world be damned because you, I mean we, are soaring freely above it all.

"WERE WOMEN MEANT TO DO EVERYTHING – WORK AND HAVE BABIES?"

Candice Bergen, American Actress
Motherhood, A Gift of Love

Chapter II
What This Guide Can Do For You

The National Association of Women Business Owners reported in 1995 that there are over 6.5 million women business owners in the U.S. who employ 11 million workers. This is more than the combined Fortune 500 companies employ worldwide, and more women are joining this quiet revolution every day. It is predicted that by the year 2000, one-half of all U.S. small businesses will be owned by women. These would-be women entrepreneurs are facing great uncertainties, particularly in light of the fact that women endure a 20% drop in income upon becoming entrepreneurs while their male counterparts, in contrast, increase their income. As a consequence, female entrepreneurs earn a shocking 50% less than their male counterparts. Moreover, women entrepreneurs and those women aspiring to become business owners are struggling with how to restructure their lives and priorities in this new independent arena.

All enterprising women must balance home and work, but those working for others have the least likelihood of success. An estimated 50% of all employed women are either somewhat or grossly dissatisfied with working due to "difficulties in juggling home and work obligations". This is in sharp contrast to women entrepreneurs who enjoy the control that they have over their lives and especially their ability to balance home and work responsibilities.

The Art Of Being An Entrepreneurial Woman seeks to inspire, encourage, and guide women contemplating entrepreneurship who also wish to be self-sufficient while enjoying fulfilling family lives. This book concentrates less on fame and big fortunes and more on self-sufficiency, balance, happiness, devotion to spending time with family and mastery of life through independence. It will show the would-be woman entrepreneur how to make the equivalent of her past salary in half the time, thereby providing her the opportunity to have ample time for her family.

This book speaks to the heart of American women regardless of their current stature in the business world. It is addressed to the millions of women who have chosen to or must work, This guide implores you to work for yourself and pay yourself what you deserve while giving concrete, proven methods on how to accomplish this. But there is much more than money at stake here. It is a matter of good mental health, healthy functional families, allowing oneself time to have fun, and experience the thrill of being truly productive. This translates into a healthier, stronger, and better functioning society.

This book speaks to the soul of all American women, including women of color who now comprise over 20% of the female population of this country. For these women, especially, career limits are narrow and the path to success in someone else's business is particularly arduous. Less than 1 % of minority women hold top executive positions in the United States, while they make up a disproportionately high percentage of the work force. Women of color need to build their own businesses more than ever to realize their full potential.

This guide speaks to American women's pocketbooks by addressing the underlying causes that allow women to charge below market and pay themselves too little. This book strives to strengthen a woman's sense of professional worth, vision, self-esteem, and sense of purpose. In addition, this book provides practical, proven advice on how to present their business in such a way as to command the going rate for products and services.

Women need to know that they have a choice. They no longer just have the option of going to school, getting a good job, working hard, hoping for a promotion or a raise and being continually disappointed ... but rather, going to school, starting a business, working hard, giving themselves a raise and being fulfilled. Would-be women entrepreneurs need to know they can choose this option and still have ample time to spend with their families which is something most careers cannot provide.

This book speaks to all enterprising women -- the secretary capable of starting a desktop publishing business; the nurse capable of contract in-home care for the elderly; the sales clerk capable of building a direct sales business; the retired teacher who wants to build a gift shop business. In other words, **The Art Of Being An Entrepreneurial Woman** reaches out to the many millions of "everyday" women who every day of their working lives wonder about the possibilities of self-sufficiency, but have no source of encouragement and realistic guidance. All too often the media hypes the Harvard MBAs recent rise to millionaire status or the get-rich-quick stories of legendary entrepreneurs. Many of these successes, of course, did not happen over-night, and many of these entrepreneurs had a great deal of help from well-connected family members or extraordinary wealth. The rest of us need to know that the things that made America great in the past are the same things that can continue to keep us great today. It is the millions of tiny businesses that no one will ever read about in Working Woman Magazine, or see on television. But all these put together comprise the healthy, productive enterprises that support our economy and the families of America.

This message steps in concert with the large American corporations because as they streamline, the trend is toward more contract labor to minimize overhead. Any well-run small business that conveniently offers competitively priced products and services will be welcomed and save the larger firms expensive overhead. In addition, a well-structured woman- owned business could have some advantages in the face of political and ethical forces that shape sub-contracting decisions.

This book speaks to the marrow of American society, our children. Three out of five Americans believe our children are suffering in two-career families because the commute, long hours, and overtime required by many employers simply leave little time for the children. In just thirty years the number of latch key children has risen 30%, leaving millions of children with no parent or adult figure at home with them after school.

Further, women need to know that as the owner of a small business they can often work at home and be there when their children come home from school. Children can also go to the office or shop and help with the business in a productive way, thereby teaching them valuable first-hand lessons which will empower them to make the best career choices for their futures.

In addition, the right entrepreneurial choice will allow ample time for adult relationships. Friendships, marriage partners or "significant others" require quality time in order for the relationships to remain healthy. This book will address how to re-prioritize and use extra time gained from earning income efficiently to re-vitalize adult relationships. All the relationship books in the world will not strengthen those bonds without devoting the necessary time on a consistent basis.

The Art Of Being An Entrepreneurial Woman strives to empower the embittered and broken; those women who have been struck down by misfortune need to know that developing mastery of life skills can heal such wounds. Dr. Kenneth Pelletier, author of Sound Mind, Sound Body, believes "...broken bones do heal strongest. Illness, limitation, suffering, poverty, isolation -- may awaken us to a deeper meaning of life." He goes on to explain that by developing independence and exerting personal control over ones life provides the wellspring for optimal mental and physical health.

This book provides practical, proven methods for small business owners to become and stay competitive as well as guidelines for restructuring priorities and redefining relationships. It gives specific guidelines on how to structure fee schedules, develop loyal clientele, price products, as well as providing a sample business plan, and step-by-step counsel on revamping one's priorities in life to get the aspiring woman entrepreneur moving on her idea immediately. In short, The Art Of Being An Entrepreneurial Woman may well be the catalyst for aspiring and practicing women entrepreneurs to gain their own measure of independence, wealth, and power.

Someone wise once said, "If you don't know where you are going -- you will end up somewhere else." Well a corollary to this might be, "If you don't know where you have been -- you can't possibly know where you are!"

As I look over my shoulder, I see many sheroes in our herstory (not history) that I am thankful for. Susan B. Anthony spent essentially her entire life of eighty-six years fighting for women's suffrage but she never lived to see the voting laws changed. Margaret Sanger worked tirelessly for thirty years so working class women would have the right to information on birth control.

1995 marks the seventy fifth anniversary of the passing of the 19th Amendment that gave women the right to vote.....***just one lifetime ago***. Perhaps even more sobering is the realization that 1995 marks the fifty ninth anniversary of the legalization of birth control.....***less than one lifetime ago***.

And now, granddaughters of America, we have opened another chapter of the woman's movement. It will be up to us to write the end of this story.

Those of you who followed the news coverage on the 1995 United Nations Conference on Women may know that of the one hundred thirty nine countries represented, twenty sent men - not women.

As the delegates from around the globe contemplated the future of women, journalist, Allison Adato reported in the October, 1995 issue of Life Magazine: "The problem is simply this. Women do not run the world. If the lives of women are to improve, the world's men must agree to the provisions laid out in the declaration for change... And not just heads of state, but fathers and husbands; neighbors and brothers; employers and religious leaders. The show is over. The work begins."

Few would argue that men of the world need to change but the solution , the work that needs to begin, begins with us -- women. It begins with each of us, one grandmother, one mother, one daughter, one female business owner, and one female supervisor -- at a time.

The journalist's comments remind me of an earlier time when Gloria Steinam and followers held an antagonistic and separatist agenda. The feminist movement, as it was euphemistically called, bemoaned our very femaleness and revolved around a divisive platform - women vs. men; us vs. them. While ironically it prescribed a future for enterprising women that was simply a carbon copy of how men strive for success. Those of us who followed this male pattern of success oftentimes began to lose our very selves. Some of us lost our husbands; many of us lost our children. Still others, lost the chance to bear children at all. Is this how modern women define success? When did becoming a successful woman begin to mean we had no families? When did becoming a successful woman begin to mean we had no one to share our lives with?

My message is not a divisive one but one of "coming together". It is my fervent hope that women <u>and</u> men along with their families shall take a front seat of importance once again in our modern world to ensure a better future for us all.

"THE MOTHER IS THE MOST PRECIOUS POSSESSION OF THE NATION, SO PRECIOUS THAT SOCIETY ADVANCES ITS HIGHEST WELL-BEING WHEN IT PROTECTS THE FUNCTIONS OF THE MOTHER."

Ellen Key (1849-1926) Swedish Writer
Motherhood, A Gift of Love

Chapter III
A Free Woman's Secrets of Success

From Nightmare to American Dream

The summer I was 15, I could lean out my bedroom window and watch Detroit's inner city burning down around me. I could hear the crack of gunfire, see columns of smoke and watch gangs of looters pick through gutted stores. As a child of the ghetto, I was not a part of the American dream. Rather, I was part of the American nightmare.

At 44, my nightmare seems to be over. I now live far from the ghetto. After spending fifteen years in what many literally refer to as paradise (Hawaii), I am now a new resident of the Yosemite foothills. With its massive oak trees, beautiful bass filled lakes, rolling hills, deer, coyote, and other wildlife -- this is just another kind of paradise. I own my own company, have authored three books and contributed to a fourth. I have become internationally known as a professional speaker, featured in a video training program sold world-wide, received Hawaii's Career Woman of the Year Award, and selected for "Who's Who Among Rising Young Americans."

I have shared my "secrets of success" with America's women entrepreneurs for over twenty years. I started speaking out on self-sufficiency through entrepreneurship even before I finished college. As the first African-American woman to graduate with a Mechanical Engineering degree from Michigan State University in 1974, I made television and large-scale conference appearances when I was only a freshman in college to inspire women and ethnic minorities to achieve high levels of success. Now I do it every day through my consulting practice. I coach would-be and brand-new women entrepreneurs all over the country each and every day of my working life. Through my books and video training programs, I coach women all around the world with insights on how to become financially independent through entrepreneurship. Here are **The Art Of Being An Entrepreneurial Woman**'s Secrets of Success. Some are simple kernels of wisdom that stand-alone. Others may require you to do some soul searching and research to define your own path. Others will be expanded on later in this guide, especially issues that center on independence, wealth, and power.

Secret #1 Living By Their Rules Means You Fail

Unless you are a male of European descent, you can pretty much forget most of the so-called rules or success. Think about it. The current "rules of corporate life" dictate a successful business woman be either childless or a stranger to whatever children she manages to squeeze out between meetings. If you win this game, what have you really won? In addition, the current "rules" dictate women must work harder than their male counterparts do to get the same position as Mr. Right. If you play this game, what do you really stand to lose? We've heard all of this enough; maybe it's time to believe it and make changes in our lives.

Nearly every rule of business life runs contrary to a woman's natural rhythms. When women commit to a fifty-week work schedule for their first five years of employment with only two weeks of vacation each year right out of college, what they are really saying is as follows.

> "No, I do not plan to have any children for five years. Moreover, I plan to bypass my most potentially successful childbearing years from the ages of twenty-two to twenty-seven. I recognize that my most fertile years to be from sixteen to twenty-seven, and by virtue of attending college have forgone my teen years and now wish to extend into what may be for some, the last-chance years to conceive and bear children."

Clearly, when making employment commitments to corporate employers, women by and large do not recognize the potential sacrifices they are, in fact, making. Moreover, sacrifices of this magnitude are virtually non-existent for men making the identical commitments. This has been due, in part, to the fact that until recently, women were simply herded on "fast forward" to pursue their careers by educators, the media, family members, and even spouses. Few stopped to share the potential downside to these endeavors; perhaps, as the first army of female corporate recruits marched into battle, few even knew.

Now it is clear, 25% of all women over thirty-five face some form of infertility. It is considered a worldwide epidemic, even in countries like India and China where there are also paradoxically, over-population concerns. This epidemic finds itself at the core of well-educated, highly ambitious, highly productive women. Women who felt they were preparing themselves as ideal role models for the next generation. How was anyone to know these women might not bear a next generation?

A senior executive told Fortune magazine in 1990, "I would never want my mother to know how much it hurts me to be childless." And finally, the two million-dollar a year achiever, Connie Chung, announces to the world and makes front-page news in 1991 with her deepest wish, "I want to have a baby!"

Ironically, once you have chosen the corporate route and dedicate yourself to fully participating, women find themselves in a day-by-day political football game whereby they are rarely passed the ball and fume silently on the benches.

In addition, it is now commonly accepted that men and women communicate differently. The pop culture chimes this message in books like the one written by John Gray, Ph.D., who wrote the runaway national best seller, Women Are From Venus and Men Are From Mars. To make matters worse, the way men communicate garners promotions while the way women communicate garners harmony. Well, pass the bacon and play the music. Ladies, isn't it is time to become self-sufficient as the owner of your own business?

Secret #2 Bypass The Heartache

Simply put -- it "ain't worth it. As a talented enterprising woman, you have already endured a lifetime of pressures that would squash the typical American male in seconds. How often do you get the benefit of the doubt, look the part, work doubly hard for a raise, and still end up under appreciated if not, resented?

Linda Chavez, Director of the Center for Equal Opportunity, a Washington-based think tank, and former director of public liaison in the Reagan administration explains:

> "Climbing to the top of the corporate world often entails cutthroat competition involving 80 and 90 hour work weeks, frequent moves and a fanatical devotion to the job above all else. Few women are willing to play by those rules for long -- thankfully so.

> The choice to have children in the first place often dramatically affects a woman's career. One study of female MBA's who took time off to have children and later returned to work found they earned 17 percent less than a comparable group of women who experienced no break in service. The study also found that only 44 percent of the first group reached senior middle-management positions, while 60 percent of those who stayed on the job reached that level."

This is a catch 22 for women; "damned, if you do and damned, if you don't." What a way to live your life. Pulitzer prize winning author, Alice Walker captures the spirit of this dilemma.

> "I think every soul is to be cherished, that every flower is to bloom. That is a very different world view from what we've been languishing under, where the thought is that the only way I can bloom is if I step on your flower, the only way I can shine is if I put out your light." (I Dream A World, by Brian Lanker, Workman Publishing, 1989.)

Imagine for a moment that like the mythical phoenix, you rise out of the ashes renewed and ready to soar. Go ahead and have your babies, but this time, bypass the heartache; don't fly back into the fire! There is a better way. Work for yourself.

Secret #3 Be Human First

While others may pre-judge you and put you in a box -- don't do it to yourself. You are first and foremost, a human being -- so start acting like one. This means transcending race and sex in your own mind. I'm fond of saying, "If you don't believe it, no one else will." This holds true whether you are marketing a product, acquiring venture capital for your business, or deciding to enjoy life as a human first. This attitude will open doors and creates opportunities otherwise unavailable. Once I started being a human being first, I was able to "see" my future husband of another race.... and conduct business with people of every conceivable nationality all across the United States and even abroad. When you speak to the heart and soul of humankind, the whole world opens up to you.

To adopt an attitude of self-awareness is not just another philosophical mind game; it is a prescription for a well balanced, purposeful life. It is an attitude that can become a source of inner wisdom and truth. Quickly you "forget" about the corporate world, educators, family pressures, the media, and even spousal demands and begin to develop a unique vision for your own life. This vision of your own life transcends all the needs and wants of business commitments and must come first. Only after you know where you want your life to go can you make the best commitments in personal or business matters.

In addition, adopting an attitude guided by inner wisdom and truth provides the backdrop to redefine every standard, milestone, goal, and aspiration you may have. It also gives you a better perspective on what constitutes appropriate time frames for each achievement. And all of this is coming from within you and not some external panel of judges who haven't a clue as to what it is you have chosen to accomplish.

Secret #4 If You Are Going To Work That Hard, Work For Yourself

Women work harder any way; women of color have to work harder still.. If you are going to work that hard, why not work for yourself?

Why would anyone prefer to work hard and pray for a raise when you could take the same time and less energy to build a business and pay yourself a raise? Oh, and every few days or so, you can take the opportunity to look yourself in the mirror and say, "Way to go!". Who needs a boss?

Often the need to work for someone else is done so to gain a false sense of security. People choose to believe that if they are good workers for X number of years, then they will be guaranteed a job and pension for the rest of their lives. The turmoil of the nineties has taught us this isn't so when even the once mighty giants of industry began to topple, (IBM, AT &T, GM) unable to afford to provide even for their once cherished white collar workers. Starting in the late nineteen eighties, IBM had to abandon their "full employment policy" for the first time in their history.

Moreover, any security that was promised was false all along. The very nature of capitalism itself relies on centuries old dictums of profit and loss which require lay-offs as a natural ebb and flow of business cycles. The arrogance of our corporate leaders to create "full employment policies" is appalling when you consider the massive numbers of people in the workforce who were led to believe them and thereby constructed life plans around such false promises. Indeed, Germain Greer said it best when she explained, "Security is when everything is settled, when nothing can happen to you; ***security is the denial of life***."

Perhaps another reason people work so hard for others is an age-old need to "perform and be reaffirmed of our abilities." We see this need in young children who work doubly hard for their teacher; or the young athlete who will go the distance for their coach. This need to be reaffirmed runs deeply through our psyches but what beats in the heart of every person seeking true fulfillment in life is a far greater need for self-affirmation. After all, when it is time to "meet your maker", one's life unfolds before you and your God -- no one else. In addition, the self-affirming individual knows that true mastery of life can only come from within; the ultimate is to become the Teacher, the Coach, and the Master of oneself.

So, take all the would-be wasted energy to appease the "false-gods" of the corporate world and channel that into your uniquely designed self-affirming, productive life. There is no need to work any harder, just most wisely... work for yourself.

Secret #5 Pass It On To Your Children

Think DYNASTY...and you have captured the idea. The light bulb on this one first went off for me about fifteen years ago while listening to an Amway presentation which "allowed the proceeds of future sales to be passed on to your children". While I chose not to get involved with that particular opportunity, I must say that the notion of building something that could continue and benefit my children really stayed with me. When you become successful in your own business you create a "money machine" that can crank out profits for many lifetimes. And what a driving force! Rather than trying to get excited about the pet project of your manager who is buried ten layers from the top -- you can continue to be excited every day of your business life about your children and their future. This connection will empower you to literally work miracles.

Secret #6 Gain Optimal Mental And Physical Health

Someone wise once said, "Hard work never hurt anyone." Well, let's take that a few steps further. Hard work can ***heal.*** In fact, those who have been struck down by misfortune need to know that developing mastery of life skills will give them a better outlook on life. Instead of only spending time with your shrink or worse, wallowing in your pain -- get to work building a business and you shall build a better life.

Dr. Kenneth Pelletier, author of Sound Mind, Sound Body, believes, "...broken bones do heal strongest. Illness, limitation, suffering, poverty, isolation -- may awaken us to a deeper meaning of life." He goes on to explain that by developing independence and exerting personal control over ones life provides the wellspring for optimal mental and physical health. He elaborates on numerous case studies of highly successful individuals who had to overcome seemingly insurmountable odds to achieve success including serious emotional obstacles.

I, for one, can testify that as the child of not one, but two alcoholics who were verbally abusive -- entrepreneurship was a big part of the "answer". I was raised in a neighborhood where crime, multi-generational welfare dependency, teen-age pregnancies, alcohol and drug addictions, high school dropouts, and functional illiteracy were an accepted part of life. Further, as a survivor of multiple sexual assaults and other crimes, I have always chosen not to become a victim. Each of us must choose. Enterprise or be victimized; it is your choice.

Secret #7 Don't Try To Have It All Because Less Is Better

This is your life. You get to pick what you want from the buffet. Choose carefully and with no regrets. If you select entrepreneurship you will be choosing a life of challenge and enterprise while allowing ample time for health, family, and fun. As an independent business owner you will call the shots on when, where, and how you spend your time. Time, after all, is not only the most precious thing in this life; it is the ***only*** thing. For how you spend your time and whom you choose to spend it with, provide the experiences that make up your life.

So, who needs a sixty (plus!) hour a week job, relentless deadlines, a boss who doesn't appreciate you fully, and a company that can't imagine you at the top when you can have a flexible schedule, time with your husband and children, more money earned in less time, and a "money machine" to pass on to your children through entrepreneurship?

Secret #8 It's Not How Much Money You Earn; It's How Much Money You Keep

I first heard this simple notion from a "termite" insurance salesperson that sold me a term life insurance policy offered by the new insurance guru of the mid-nineteen eighties, A.L. Williams. Williams developed an insurance company that specialized in term life insurance because he felt that most insurance companies misled the average person by encouraging them to buy whole life insurance which provided woefully inadequate settlements for overpriced premiums. Term life insurance, on the other hand, costs substantially less and provides significantly higher payouts for the premiums charged. His prescription to achieve financial independence at least in part, was to buy "term and invest the difference". While I listened to the "termite insurance salesperson", something clicked inside. For the first time in my life, I began examining my own program to achieve financial independence and found that just a few immediate, simple changes made a big difference long term.

Pay yourself first, invest your money wisely, and live within your means are just a few of the dictums I began to strive for each and every day. Perhaps more compellingly, I encouraged our oldest son (now eleven) to do the same and watched as the years flew by, how this young child began to amass a small fortune.

Secret # 9 Develop A Strong Support Structure

I can still remember hearing the collective cheers roar out when A Woman of Substance first appeared as a mini-series nearly a decade ago. It was based on Barbara Taylor Bradford's novel, which had become a national best seller. The main character, Emma Harte, began life as a chambermaid and ended it as an extraordinarily wealthy entrepreneur and owner of a successful business conglomerate. But, here's the catch. Emma Harte made this incredible 'rags to riches' journey -- all by herself. She also abandoned her first born, alienated most of those who worked for her, and even delegated child rearing to the extent that her own sons felt vengeful and plotted to kill her. Granted, this is a piece of fiction, but I feel it is telling that such a male-oriented female would become a fictional shero to literally millions of enterprising women.

Women need not aspire to such an empty life in order to have wealth and success in the business world. In fact, many experts believe that "people who need people" live longer, are more productive, and are happier with their lives. Finally, a rhythm that resonates with the spirit of womanhood has become a recognized advantage in creating a successful life.

Indeed, build a support structure of people you care about and that care about you. Don't try to do it alone. Moreover, you, unlike the fictional Emme Harte, will find strength in your relationships. This strength is power that will serve to inspire you with purpose and invigorate your spirit when the inevitable challenges of life seem insurmountable.

Secret #10 Help Others and Success Will Come

Often those of us who are scarred from our battles in life, feel inadequate and begin a lifelong process of repairing the damage that's been done. In so doing, some of us, forget to live. We get so involved in the process of fixing ourselves that we wander around on emotional crutches accustomed to sympathy and comfortable with playing the victim.

Well, I for one, had plenty to fix. But if I had let the pain from my past consume me through a continuous preoccupation with self-help books, support groups, therapy sessions, and the like, there would be little time left to live. Fortunately, I paid an appropriate amount of attention to my emotional baggage, got the help I needed, and moved on.

Ironically, it was the moving on to strive to help others that proved to be the best mechanism for healing. Moreover, I was able to incorporate this "helping" in the form of not only volunteer work but as fee for service work as an independent business consultant. In addition, I found myself talking primarily to women and women of color. I shared with them the importance of mastering ones life through mastering ones business endeavors. I helped women learn to become independent. And when these women found their independence in business, often they found much more: prosperity, time to nurture loving adult relationships, ample time for children, time for spiritual growth and even time to nurture their own physical vitality. In short, these women, like myself, found success through entrepreneurship meant success in life -- it meant true freedom.

Secret #11 Buy Low and Sell High

I was dreaming one night and as dreams would have it, a truism emerged like a chant as I awoke from a deep sleep: **Buy Low -- Sell High**. At first I thought I was in the middle of a stock market investment seminar but I began to reflect on the bits and pieces of my dream and realized how this kernel of wisdom holds true for most money-making ventures.

Obviously, when you buy something at a low price and later sell it for more than you paid for it, you have made money. Granted, inflation and tax ramifications complicate this overly simplistic analysis but few would argue that as a general rule of thumb, whenever you buy low and sell high, you make a profit.

And yet, how many of us violate this very rule that makes such good common sense. For example, most people are afraid to invest in the stock market. Moreover, if they do give it a try they will usually wait until the stocks they have been considering show a definite trend upwards and jump on the band wagon along with everyone else. This, of course, is right when the market experiences an "adjustment" and the very trend you thought you had spotted has subsequently made national news. Lo and behold, panic strikes and the novice investor loses again as she sells her declining stock and does the exact opposite of what common sense would dictate.

How many people buy brand new cars and then sell them once they are four or five years old? How many of us buy our primary residence after the neighborhood is established, the roads are already widened, and the house is picture perfect and ready to move in? Time and time again, most people pay top dollar for their assets and minimize or forfeit all together any profits they might otherwise experience. In contrast, when you buy stocks after the prices have fallen; buy a two year old car after it has taken its biggest drop in depreciation; buy a "fixer upper" in a newly-discovered area before everyone else has it figured out and thus driven up the housing prices -- you maximize your chances of gaining a profit. Why not take advantage of this simple truism? It can make a world of difference in a single lifetime. If you pass this thinking on to your children, your family will benefit for generations to come.

From an entrepreneurial point of view, one of the easiest ways to make money is to find a good product, negotiate a low wholesale price and sell the item at retail. If your business is otherwise solidly based, you can typically double, triple, or quadruple your money. For those of us who sell our time, we get 1,440 "free" minutes everyday from which we can offer our clients. We must simply marry our talent with the right kind of service business; one that commands $35 to over $200 per hour. Remember to always buy low and sell high.

Secret # 12 Simplify, Focus, and Execute

This credo has helped thousands of my "students", as well as myself to make the most of our professional time. Unfortunately, most people spend too much time "sweating" the details and fret much of their time away. Fear robs us of the present. The most important things you can do once your vision, plans, and priorities are in place are to simplify, focus, and execute your plan one step at a time beginning right now.

In summary, these "Secrets of Success" have guided others and me in our search for a more purposeful life that beats with the rhythms of our womanliness. They are intended to be an overview of top threads for a much richer tapestry. In order for you to achieve true freedom, however, you may need to adopt a completely new approach to life.

"IF I ASSUME THAT THERE IS NOTHING I CAN DO TO CHANGE MYSELF OR MY SITUATION, THEN CHANCES ARE, NOTHING WILL CHANGE."

Beth Wilson Saavedra
Meditations for New Mothers

Chapter IV
A Free Woman's Complete Approach To Life

"To be somebody, a woman does not have to be more like a man, but has to be more of a woman."

Sally Shaywitz "Catch 22 for Mothers"
The New York Times, March 4, 1975

Who Is Truly Free?

My father always said, "The only free people in this world are white men and black women." I grew to have some understanding of what he meant with this often mentioned colorful remark. Life taught me that European-descent American men ***make the rules***; African-descent American women devoid of any societal expectations, could ***break all rules***.

Few would argue the vast majority of written history, business protocol, and even business dress code were created by European descent males and most would agree their potential for success is higher than any other identifiable group in America. Indeed, how can one fail when you are the favored track star running your best venue with a home team audience and you also happen to be the judge holding the yardstick and the stop watch, as well?

In contrast, African American women have been cast in the lowest images... every expectation reduced to such lows that any achievement, however small would be deemed a success. Indeed, how can one fail if no one assumes you can succeed at anything? It would be a little like running your heart out at a track meet with no yardstick, stop watch or any audience for that matter, and knowing that all the judges are blind.

Perhaps W.E. DuBois said it best when he wrote that every African American inhabits, "a world that yields him no true self-consciousness, but only lets him see himself through the revelations of the other world."

The total lack of positive societal expectations made me search for my own inner awareness. With no standards of excellence provided for me, I had to come up with my own. With no audience cheering me on, I had to learn a quiet acceptance of my own achievements. With judges totally blind to my successes, I had to learn to judge, critique, and praise my own work. With no patterns in life to follow, I had to find my own way. And in the end, I found true freedom.

A New Pattern of Success For All Women

This must now be your quest. I encourage all women; women of every race and class to recast their patterns of success because to some degree we have all been provided the wrong expectations. Women will find freedom as an entrepreneur only after we find freedom from all the strings that bind us. Women have been running on the wrong track. Perhaps, we shouldn't be running in "this race" at all. We have certainly relegated our yardsticks, and stopwatches to the wrong judges and have played away from the home team for far too long. It is time to come home.

And home is where the very heart of civilization resides. It is where not only great men but great women are nurtured and taught the ways of good citizenship, worthwhile scholarly pursuits, enjoyable athletic endeavors, spiritual connectedness, the importance of marriage and family, and much, much, more. The keepers of the hearth can and have been the very keepers of civilization.

Philosopher George Bernard Shaw once commented, "Perhaps the greatest social service that can be rendered by anybody to the country and to mankind is to bring up a family." ...To bring up a solid, well-nurtured family is the first step to having a solid, well-nurtured society. A strong marriage yields a strong foundation to raise strong, emotionally healthy children who are well equipped to contribute positively to society. The collective contributions of these strong and healthy people, in turn, strengthen the community, our nation, and finally -- our world.

I realize this is a decidedly different point of few. We have concerned ourselves almost exclusively with the products from good homes that we have forgotten how important the good homemakers are. We emphasize the great "student's success" and forget about the influence of great teachers. It is the diplomat, scientist, businessperson, physician, or attorney that receives all of the applause. And it is their first teachers, who are most often their mothers, who go unheralded. Moreover, the history writers have been predominantly male, and it is their perspective that is best illustrated in their accounts of great achievement. The fact that few women are held in high esteem in these chronicles of success, should be of little consequence to women. It is up to ***us*** to write our own journals, to find our own "sheroes", and to chronicle our own "herstories".

Modern Women Have Lost Touch With Their Womanhood

Unfortunately, women have lost their way. Modern women are caught up in overextended lifestyles and achievement-oriented values that reflect men, not women. Women have lost the mirrors to their souls.

Judith Durek, author of Circle of Stones, is a psychotherapist and leads small groups of women in retreat settings to assist them in getting in touch with their womanhood. She expresses this lost need of women to construct their own patterns of success as follows. The poetic form in which Durek expresses modern woman's search for womanhood resonates like a chant:

> " How might your life have been different if there had been a place for you ... a place of women, where you where received and affirmed? A place where other women, perhaps somewhat older, had been affirmed before you, each in her time, affirmed, as she struggled to become more truly herself.
>
> A place where, after the fires were lighted, and the drumming , and the silence, there would be a hush of expectancy filing the entire chamber... a knowing that each woman there was leaving old conformity to find herself... a sense that all womanhood stood on a threshold.
>
> And if, during the hush, the other women, slightly older, had helped you to trust your own becoming ... to trust it and quietly and prayerfully to nurture it. **How might *your life* be different**?"

What if you were encouraged by your elders to examine several patterns of life that rang true for the female spirit and was in keeping with your natural rhythms of life: the rhythms that call you to conceive, bear, and raise children; nurture husbands and create a home; explore intellectual pursuits to expand not only your own minds but the minds of the future; create wealth and prosperity by way of example to inspire those around you; to follow the ebb and flow of your cycles with patience, faith, and conviction.

What if you were convinced that one particular pattern that allowed you to be true to your womanhood provided both money and freedom and was one that included entrepreneurship? And what if you were convinced that this pattern provided you ample time at home and with you family, a flexible work schedule that you controlled, and significant income? And while this pattern differed wildly from the "traditional standards", you would continue to pursue this pattern because you knew it was right for you.

Women's Current Options For Success

When we reflect for a moment on the options provided to modern enterprising women, the patterns of success merely mimic what has traditionally worked well for men. Women are encouraged to go to college, get their MBA, and work for someone else fifty-two weeks a year for twenty-five years. Then, we take a vacation for only two to six weeks, and are "on call" for any business trip deemed necessary regardless of family obligations. For the ambitious, come to work early (7:00 a.m.) and leave late (7:00 p.m.) to make the absolute best impression, while working on projects that hopefully line up to some extent with your enterprising objectives. Then, women expect to receive titles and accolades commensurate with their abilities but instead receive a reluctant "peer group's" evaluation that always falls short of a woman's true merits. Oh, and if you manage to squeeze out any children in between meetings, you get six to eight weeks of unpaid leave that is be grudgingly handed out as if this time is "lost and unproductive". Even though womansense would tell you that you really need more time with your infants, you find yourself at the center of some useless debate about a "mommy track".

New Patterns of Success For Women

In contrast, what if you go to college, get your MBA., get three to five years of initial corporate experience, get married, start a home-based consulting practice charging competitive rates of $100 to $200 per hour, develop a schedule that allows you time to enterprise on projects that truly excite your intellect while leaving ample time for a serious hobby (go ahead and bike across America -- you will have both the time and the money). When you feel its time to have your babies, save up enough ahead of time to pay any bills for four to six months after they are born so that you are home with your infants. Then schedule yourself part-time until the children are in school so that you feel you are always "there" for them. (What you will find is that you will be able to earn just as much part-time, if not more income, than in a traditional full-time corporate position.) Nurture your husband who may well be one the traditional track; make your home a true respite from his times in the trenches. Enjoy creating family traditions and relish in the fact that at least one of you can always be home for spring, Christmas, and summer break. Put President, Executive Director, or Senior Partner on your business card and pat yourself on the back whenever you need it. Ask your clients to write you letters of appreciation and build an affirming portfolio over a lifetime of mutually beneficial working relationships. Be the primary influence in your children's lives in an everyday "real" sense. Once they are old enough, engage them in the business. Take them with you to assist at trade shows, give them paid duties that they can proudly accomplish, let them earn as they learn invaluable lessons about entrepreneurship and self-sufficiency. And when its time to enjoy leisurely pursuits, take the kids with you the next time you ride a century (bike 100 miles in one day) and let them surprise you at how far they can go.

Does this "pattern" seem idyllic and unrealistic to you? Does this lifestyle seem far removed from the cruel twists and turns of "real" life? Well ladies, I am proud to say that this pattern is a true reflection of my own life and I take full credit in making it as much a manifestation of my dreams as the real world will allow. This vision for my lifestyle began deep inside as I struggled to find a pattern of success that pulsed **with** the beat of my womanliness -- not against it.

Entrepreneurism -- A Way of Life

I call this pattern of success **Entrepreneurism** . Entrepreneurism is a philosophy of self-sufficiency. It is the vision that one can create prosperity from one's own mastery of life skills; it is the wisdom that one can "create something from nothing".

Indeed, the first time a woman holds her newborn child, she has a visceral experience that tells her in no uncertain terms that she (with the help of her partner) created "something from nothing". In that sense, women have a psychological edge over men. We have a knowingness of certain abstract notions. We can feel our way through situations and submerge our egos sufficiently to gain confidences, build rapport, and ultimately construct businesses.

Entrepreneurism is nothing more than choosing to exercise control over ones enterprising activities vs. relinquishing control of the fruits of ones labor over to someone else. In addition, Entrepreneurism embodies a spirit of taking control over all the key areas of your life; spiritual development, physical health, family life, avocations, personal/private time, time with your spouse, and more.

With half of all employed women are either somewhat or grossly dissatisfied with working due to "difficulties in juggling home and work obligations", it becomes a compelling challenge to examine alternatives. Women entrepreneurs, on the other hand, enjoy the control they have over their lives and especially their ability to balance home and work responsibilities.

The scientific and medical communities have long sensed a person's need to maintain control over one's life as a precursor to the very essence of life... optimal physical health. It is as if our minds control our mental health and in turn, manifests our physical health. This occurs whether we choose to be conscious of it or not. Perhaps the mechanisms at work in Entrepreneurism and the highly researched new field of psychoneuroimmunology are one and the same.

Psychoneuroimmunology encompasses the mind and emotions (psycho), the brain and central nervous system (neuro), and the body's cellular defenses against abnormal internal cells or external invaders such as bacteria or viruses (immunology). In only ten years, research from this new field has established a correlation between high levels of stress and a myriad of health problems. These include cardiovascular disease, high blood pressure, headaches, back pain, ulcers, anxiety, chronic fatigue syndrome, depression, alcohol and drug abuse, suicide, increased susceptibility to infectious disease, auto immune disorders, and even the common cold.

Clearly, taking control of ones life by adopting Entrepreneurism can reduce stress and will subsequently lead to enhanced mental and physical health. The decision to take on a life style of self-sufficiency has much more at stake than most of us would have allowed ourselves to believe even a decade ago.

Dr. Kenneth Pelletier, author of Sound Mind, Sound Body has observed, " For centuries doctors and scientists have attempted to determine a direct causal relationship between emotions, behaviors, and mental attitudes on the one hand and human health and illness on the other. In the second century A.D. the Greek physician Galen noted that 'melancholic' women seemed to have a higher incidence of cancer." Who hasn't admitted to "making oneself sick" on occasion. Intuitively, we know what the medical and scientific communities have been groping to prove for eons. Writing in the *Southern Medical Journal* in 1986, Dr. John F. Hiatt of the University of the California School of Medicine in San Francisco drew these conclusions from his research and clinical practices,

> "The spiritual dimension is that part of the person concerned with meaning, and is therefore a principal determinant of health-related attitudes."

Moreover, Pelletier makes it clear that from his four-year study of fifty-three extraordinarily successful individuals (including Norman Cousins, Paul Hawkens, Lindsay Wagner, David Rockefeller, and John Sculley), that in order to achieve a sound body, one must develop the skills to achieve a sound mind. One important key to achieving a sound mind requires the emotional fortitude to exercise control in ones life, even in the face of situations - illness, divorce, or the death of a relative - that can be overwhelming. And while clearly one must always continually distinguish between what one can and cannot control, one must always choose to exercise control in ones life. Pelletier notes, "Control is an ongoing, lifelong orientation. When the next challenge arises, return to the first step (as detailed in Sound Mind, Sound Body) and work through the stages again. With practice and over time, these steps will become virtually instantaneous, as with any practiced skill. Then you will know that control - the certainty that you can influence your life's direction - is firmly established."

Entrepreneurism is a cornerstone of success in life along with optimal mental and physical health. It allows us to listen to the rhythms of our lives and to live with room to maneuver around all the obstacles that are sure to be set in our paths.

Choosing Freedom

The courage to find a successful pattern of life lies within you and is struggling to get out. This struggle beats in the heart of every person who seeks mastery over his or her life. Deepak Chopra, author of Ageless Body, Timeless Mind, has delineated Ten Keys To Active Mastery which include, listening to your body's wisdom, taking time to meditate, relinquishing your need for external approval, replacing fear-motivated behavior with love-motivated behavior.

Listen to your body's wisdom, which expresses itself through signals of comfort and discomfort. Chopra suggests that when choosing a certain behavior, ask your body, "How do you feel about this?" If your body sends a signal of physical or emotional distress, watch out. If your body sends a signal of comfort and eagerness, proceed. Clearly, we get caught up with artificial schedules in modern day life that send signals of discomfort to our bodies which we choose to ignore. Choosing Entrepreneurism allows you to listen, make adjustments to your schedule that bring you back in touch with your body's wisdom.

Taking time to meditate allows you reconnect with your source of what Chopra calls, "pure awareness". It is what I call your woman sense; it is the part of you that knows what is right for you and your family.

When you relinquish your need for external approval, Chopra believes you alone become the judge of your worth. He feels that goal then becomes, "to discover infinite worth in yourself, no matter what anyone else thinks." He concludes, "there is great freedom in this realization." Indeed, women have long sought the approvals of others be they fathers, bosses, husbands, and even our own offspring. Women need to forget what others think of them and develop of a sense of standards from deep within that provides us the yardstick we need.

When you replace fear-motivated behavior with love-motivated behavior you are no longer plagued by the past. Chopra explains,

> "Fear is the product of memory, which dwells in the past. Remembering what hurt us before, we direct our energies toward making certain that an old hurt will not repeat itself. But trying to impose the past on the present will never wipe out the threat of being hurt. That happens only when you find the security of your own being, which is love. Motivated by the truth inside you, you can face any threat because your inner strength is invulnerable to fear."

Once you choose to forget the past and listen to the wisdom in your own heart will you be free to pursue a pattern of success for your life. Moreover, when you allow your enterprising activities to be guided by the love you have for your family, the more you will feel in charge of your life.

Mastery of life begins with the mastery of your inner self. Once you choose to be free from the strings that bind you, you are -- at once-- free.

I believe the challenges women face today must be met and overcome through having a clear vision, high self-esteem, self-sufficiency skills, a strong sense of purpose, and an absolute commitment to building their own business.

This philosophical foundation is offered to provide the roots to the tree. The branches now follow. However, the "how to" portion of this book will ring hollow indeed, unless it rests on “terra firma”. Make certain your foundation is firmly constructed in order for your life's masterpiece to rise.

"THOUGHTS...

GIVEN LIFE...

CREATE FORM."

Eva Weir
Pocketbook of Change

Chapter V
Develop Your Own Personal Vision of Your Life

I was nearly killed once and almost killed myself three times. The summer I was fifteen, I kneeled on the floor of my neighborhood's corner liquor and sundries store. A burning building from across the street splashed the evening sky with golden , red waves of fire and made me sweat as I began my search. I picked up a handful of barrettes, lotions, and shampoos and proceeded to walk out the open door without paying. Suddenly, a National Guardsman stood before me in full uniform and pointed a rifle at my chest. He yelled, "Halt, or I'll shoot!".

Only God understands what happened next. I arose, looked him straight in the eyes, clasped my stolen treasures to my chest, and ran. I felt certain the next moments which unfolded and have been played out in slow motion across the screen of my mind a million times, would be my last. You see, it was the summer of 1967, and I lived on Larchmont Street and Woodward Avenue in Detroit, Michigan, which literally burned during one of the bloodiest race riots of that era.

Indeed, one part of me was a bright, studious, hard-working, clean-cut, hopeful young human being and another part of me was the desperate, wounded, woman-child of abuse and poverty. ***But I chose the first part of me to choreograph my dance of life .***

Most casual observers would have deemed my childhood dreams as foolish and unrealistic. Despite my surroundings, I envisioned a better life: one, which included higher education, success in business, a beautiful home, and a loving family. In fact, whenever I shared my wild, fanciful dreams with others, most laughed. In addition to the typical challenges young people face when growing up, I had to somehow heal the wounds of my childhood, mature, get a college education with no family money or emotional support, and finish college in four years like everybody else. All this, even though I worked two part-time jobs, started a career, and -- in the meantime -- forgot all the negative thoughts, gestures, and hostile acts most professors, my employers and fellow-employees, new "neighbors", and classmates showered onto me each and every day of my life. You see, while I could temporarily suspend the belief of my own "well documented" stupidity, laziness, poor attitude, weak character, and criminal mindedness -- most of those around me, could not.

What sustained me and will work equally well for you, is developing your own personal vision of success for your life. It means allowing no one else's opinion of you to matter because this gift of time you have been given on the planet is your gift, alone. At first, you must disallow everyone; no one else can matter. Once you are tuned in to your personal vision, you can begin to seek out or align yourself with others. But you must come first. You have all heard the saying, "You must take care of yourself before you can take care of someone else." Well, stop thinking of others for a moment, and think only of yourself. This seemingly selfish act will allow you to get your life on track and provide the most good for those you cherish.

The concept of a personal vision goes beyond just business endeavors and starts with what you believe is your purpose in life. It extends into a mental and emotional image of how you wish to spend your personal, family, and professional time. Finally, you must design a written game plan for these key areas in your life.

A Written Game Plan Manifests Your Vision

On July 9, 1983, I constructed a written, ten-year game plan – for the **first time**. At the time, my husband and I had just filed for personal bankruptcy in the aftermath of some poor business decisions and a lackluster business climate. We were emotionally recuperating but starting over again financially seemed insurmountable. We were essentially penniless and lived from meager consulting project to meager consulting project. Our "home" was a $15.00 a day room at the downtown Honolulu YMCA which we prepaid on a daily basis. We ate cans of tuna bought on sale and cups of noodles. To complicate things further, my fifteen year old stepson lived with us at that time and we had to provide him his school supplies, money for field trips, food, clothing, and emotional support while we were ill equipped to give much of anything even to ourselves. In short, we were the classic scenarios you read about in the books on entrepreneurship: three out of five fail within the first year and the balance fail in the second. We had already crashed landed and were picking up the pieces.

Incredibly, I wrote that in ten years, I would be a nationally known author and public speaker, own a beautiful hillside home, have an eight-year-old child of my own, have a loyal national clientele, a healthy marriage, time for fun, be physically fit, and at a comfortable weight.

In three years, I wrote, I would earn six-figure income, take a trip to Europe, buy a 27-foot sailing boat, own a home, and more.

Ladies, once you seriously dedicate time and emotional energy to visionary thinking, hold onto your hats because miracles can and do happen.

In thirty days, I landed a $25,000 three-month project with the largest civilian employer in the state! In ninety days, we owned (paid in full) a 27-foot Catalina Sailboat. In six months, I had worked with our bank to re-establish our credit. In nine months we bought a townhouse. In twelve months we were on our way to Europe for a month, and I was three months pregnant with our first son. The following summer, I rode the first Bicycle Century in my life. When I completed 100 miles on my bike in one day, I knew miracles could happen. ***By year five -- not ten -- I had achieved every one of my ten-year goals!***

While I had let vague images of success sustain me in the past; these experiences helped me to discover the power of writing my goals down and creating a written game plan for my life. I would like to thank a remarkable woman who helped me to really see the wisdom in doing this, Trinidad Hunt. "Trin" convinced me (and fifty-nine other people) on that unforgettable day in 1983, that dreams can come true, and sooner than you think, if you write them down. I would like to share with you some of the key things I learned from "Trin" and other life planning gurus. Had I known and believed these truths earlier in my independent professional career, I clearly would have started soaring sooner.

Write Your Visionary Game Plan Down

1. Use the Active Voice
    - I have
    - I am
    - I own
    - I earn.

2. Be specific:
    - I own an 1800 square foot townhouse in Mililani
    - I have a contract with Acme Corp. valued at $30,000
    - I have a healthy marriage with Larry

3. Use actual dates and the age you will be at that time:
    - September 15, 1998, I am 45 years old and...

4. Start at ten years out and bring yourself back to the present:
    - Ten Year Written Plan
    - Six Year Written Plan
    - Five, Four, Three, Two, One Year Written Plan
    - Six-month, Three-month, One month, One-week Written Plan
    - One-week, One-day Written Plan

5. After you write down your visionary life plan, ask yourself if you will commit the necessary time, energy, and money to make the plan work. Now, ask your significant others in your life if they are willing to support you in achieving your life plan.

6. Prioritize your goals. I labeled my most important set of goals A1, 2, 3, etc.; my second most important set of goals B1, 2, 3, etc. In this way, if a short-term conflict arose between family and professional goals, I "knew" ahead of time that I would choose family goals first.

7. Take that first step on the first day of your plan. Remember that a journey of a thousand miles begins with one footstep. Remind yourself each and everyday that in order to achieve your ten-year plan, you must accomplish something towards it today.

8. Re-examine how far you have come at the end of each day.

9. Re-set and re-prioritize as needed with no blaming or regrets. Remember you are human -- first.

10. Celebrate your milestone achievements; Enjoy the journey.

A study of the 1953 graduates of Yale University concluded that long-term written goals make a substantial impact on career results. The graduates were asked if they had a clear, specific set of goals written down, with a plan for achieving those goals. Only three percent had such written goals.

Twenty years later, in 1973, the researchers interviewed the surviving members of the 1953 class. They discovered that the three percent with written, specific goals were worth more in financial terms than all the rest combined.

Obviously, this study measured only people's financial development. However, the interviewers also discovered that the less-measurable (or more subjective) measures such as the level of happiness and joy also were superior in the aforementioned three percent.

Conclusion: Write your plan down and get moving! When you start on the right foot, at least you know that some of the "laws of success" are on your side.

Recognize Time is More Precious Than Money

Many of you have heard the story of Queen Elizabeth I, who whispered on her deathbed, "All of the treasures of my kingdom for but a single moment in time." Time is not only the most precious commodity we have in this life -- in many ways, it is the only thing we have in this life. The time we spend is, after all, the accumulative experiences that make up our lives. When we speak of wasting "time", we are really saying that we are wasting a portion of our lives. Don't ever allow yourself this indulgence because it will eat away at your subconscious and rob you of fulfillment and fill your heart with useless regret, every moment you waste. Consequently, we must strive to live a balanced life each and every day that leaves ample time for all the people and endeavors we deem important.

Have Fun

This was an important lesson for me once I began to cherish time; began, in essence, to cherish my life. Suddenly, my life's priorities fell into place and my level of efficiency naturally rose two-fold. I found I could complete a project in half the time, send my bill and get paid as if I had labored extensively over it. This allowed me to have my oldest son in nursery school from 8:30 a.m. to 1:00 p.m., while earning more money than most professional women earn working from 8:00 a.m. to 6:00 p.m. At last, I had found my freedom; I had found my life.

I can honestly say that when it is time for my life to end, I shall have spent a gloriously rich amount of quality time with my three children and my husband of nearly two decades! In addition, I will have made a significant contribution to the business world, empowering thousands of entrepreneurs to achieve higher levels of success. I am especially proud of having struck this balance, particularly when you consider that no one, on his or her deathbed ever whispers, "Gosh, I wish I had spent more time at the office."

Chapter VI

Racism and Sexism are Figments of the Imagination

Imagine a world where sex and race have no meaning.... a world where everyone is treated with respect. Suppose you could experience what it was like to be thought of as intelligent, hard working, and dedicated to success? What would it feel like to aspire to be well traveled, well read, highly accomplished in your field and beautiful in spirit? More specifically, what would it be like to have all of the people around including your business associates, relatives, friends, clients, and managers who felt you had the utmost talent, skills, and abilities?

This world can be yours with the power of your own thoughts. While no one can change others, we all have the power to change ourselves. Once we change how we see and feel about ourselves, many around us begin to change in response to who we are and who we are becoming. Moreover, there are millions of people who needn't change at all. Contrary to popular belief, there are many good-hearted people out there that have always been open and receptive to women and women of color, in the first place.

Your Perspective Determines Who You Are

Your beliefs -- learned or imagined -- dictate the rules of your life. I had my first glimpse of the power of one's own imagined perspective on one's behavior as a young girl. My father re-told a particular incident of his childhood so frequently that I felt that I had experienced it with him. This is his story:

> When I was nine years old, I had a dear friend, David, at school. He and I were like peas in a pod. Wherever he went, I went. Whatever game I played, he played. I went to his house to play and he came to mine.
>
> Then one day, quite by accident, my friend of German ancestry was walking down the street with his mother. They were heading straight for me and my mother. As we approached each other, David hollered out, "There's Melvin and his mother."
>
> I will never forget the look of horror on David's mother's face. She "knew" for the first time, I had African ancestry by gazing upon my mother's strong ethnic features and olive complexion.

That was the last time I ever spoke to my dear "friend", David.

Every time my father told this remarkable story, I sat transfixed. How on earth could my grandmother's appearance mean the difference between someone loving my father and hating him? How could one single fact about my father; a rather coincidence of birth, determine how people would react to him? Moreover, if one moment you didn't "know" this single fact because it was otherwise invisible, and the next moment, you "found out" -- how could this alter your entire frame of mind, emotions, and actions?

You see, my dad looked Mediterranean, like his Greek immigrant father. He would have to announce his African lineage lest no one would know. Time and time again, upon the discovery of his minute African Ancestry, his life would be dramatically affected through the abrupt loss of friends, neighbors, and even jobs.

I thought about these bizarre incidences and realized how abstract the notion of race really was. If a person thought you were European American, then you could be witty, fun, attractive, intelligent - and even a coveted friend. If a person thought you were African American, then you were ignorant, ugly, mean-spirited, and a potentially dangerous enemy. The power of one's mind creates this reality and could change in an instant.

I found the concept of race and its resultant political and societal ramifications extremely complicated to understand because my own extended family looked like the United Nations. During slavery times, the "one drop rule" was established so that the children fathered by slaveholders with their African slaves would be legally considered Negro and therefore, property. But legalities aside, when a family, such as my own, has had many generations of mixed marriages, it becomes quite the trick to ascertain who is "black" and who is "white". Consequently, it took me years to fathom why different races held mutual antagonisms because from my point of view, it was rather a technicality that determined one's "race". When I finally thought I understood America's tacit race relation's policy, I embraced a kind of 70's separate but equal mentality. Shortly after that I began sporting an Afro and a pierced nose. Then I met my husband-to-be of another race. This threw me into yet another tizzy!

Indeed, I was taught the "fact" that I was Black and the menu of attributes associated with my race. But I refused to accept the negative stereotypes that came with being a Negro. Instead I filled my own head with notions of success and a middle-class lifestyle far beyond anything anyone on the planet ever dreamed for me.

As fascinating as my father's stories were, it was not until I had similar experiences that the notion of race as an imaginary concept really hit home. The further I lived and worked away from Detroit's inner city, it seemed, and the less my contemporaries saw me as "Black". It was as if I was out of context and therefore unimaginably of African ancestry. The following story illustrates.

> As a resident of Hawaii during an election year, I went to the polls to vote. Representatives of the Office of Hawaiian Affairs (OHA) approached me. OHA is a separate governing body similar to what some Native Americans have on the mainland, which oversees their homelands and cultural preservation.
>
> The Hawaiian OHA representatives asked, "Please come to our table and register to vote with us." I was confused at first. As a new resident, was I expected to be knowledgeable of Hawaiian affairs and therefore allowed to vote on measures that only affected the indigenous people?
>
> Then, all at once, I knew. These Hawaiian OHA representatives had mistaken me for one of their own. I couldn't help but be touched by the irony. Polynesian means "many races" and my United Nations family tree reflected that I was, indeed of many races. First I laughed, then I smiled, and finally tears welled up in my eyes because once again I learned, the notion of race is only what we imagine.

Develop Your Own Sense of Self

My sense of self evolved to a place of racelessness and sexlessness. I truly began to see my self as a human being -- first.

I broke new ground when I graduated from Michigan State University with my Mechanical Engineering Degree in 1974, as the first African American woman to do so. After the rigorous engineering coursework, I sailed through my two and half year MBA program in only sixteen months. I became a plant engineer, college instructor, systems analyst, manager, the youngest, the only racial minority, the first female this and that so often that I finally lost count. After all, I was a human being -- first.

By the time I married my Scottish descent husband and had our three children, my journey was complete. By now, the concept of race in my world was not only imaginary -- it was rendered obsolete.

In addition, as I observed the mind expansion that occurred within me; I could not help but notice the mind expansion that occurred within those around me. Further, I began to feel not only the changes within but also the changes from without; people behaved differently and for the better. Fortunately for my family and me, we were able to grow during an era, unlike my father, when the rest of the world was growing too.

And it is up to us, who have collectively rendered racism and sexism obsolete -- to continue to be the catalyst for more change. A change of **heart**; a change of **mind**, can happen in an instant. We need to always think not only of ourselves but also of all those around us as human beings -- first.

Imagine a world where there is no racism and sexism and you are instantly there. For those of us fortunate enough to live in the United States, we have enough laws, real societal pressures, and sanctions to back up our "imaginary world". And as we move in this new realm of human beingness, we are free to create and manifest our own personal vision of our lives. Those not ready or unwilling to imagine our world, will continue to see us stereotypically and for the most part, need not be ever dealt with.

For example, as a small business development consultant, I have approached thousands of potential clients. I realize there are those who would not hire me simply because of my gender or the color of my skin. However, I neither dwell on that "fact" nor ponder it when a prospective client declines my services. I honestly feel that their shortsightedness is their own loss since they will not allow themselves to benefit from my consulting services. In short, I don't work for such small minded people.

Conversely, every single one of my clients, by virtue of them being my clients, are open-minded and receptive to me; my expertise, God-given talents, learned skills... my human beingness.

In structuring my life in this fashion, I have summarily eliminated racism and sexism from my world and replaced these abhorrent sentiments with positive mental and emotional energy. This frees me to make the contributions to the business world I was intended to make all along. Granted, I am subject to an occasional screaming skinhead and hateful stares when out in public. In addition, I realize there are merchants and sales people who will just as soon look the other way than acknowledge my presence in a store. In the case of disrespectful merchants and clerks, however, I am more than comforted to know that I can choose to spend neither time nor money with them.

When I first left graduate school I avidly pursued my business career in corporate America. This road somehow seemed safe. When I worked for large companies like Dow Chemical and IBM, these companies had affirmative action programs ostensibly in place "to help" people like me. But what these firms' public relations departments will not tell you is that if women or people of color inadvertently align themselves with a closeted racist or sexist manager, their whole career could be jeopardized. Moreover, there are bound to be racist and sexist individuals in such organizations who invariably feel strongly that someone like myself was a mere token and undeserving of my successes.

I opted for an independent professional life so that I was free to create my own world devoid of hateful energy. When my clients bring me in, they make their vote of confidence each and every time they write me a check for my services. Over the years I have amassed a portfolio of letters of appreciation whereby my clients state specifically what they appreciate about the work and the contribution I have made to their company. In addition, they detail specific results that they attribute to my work. Thus, on any given day should I feel depressed or out of touch with a strong sense of self-worth, I need go no further than my letter of appreciation file to reconnect with my ***imaginary*** world. Or is it my real world? I think you and I both know the answer.

"MUCH AS I RESPECTED THE AUTHORITY OF MY MASTER, I COULD NOT REMAIN SILENT ON A SUBJECT THAT SO DEARLY CONCERNED ME. ONE DAY, WHEN I INSISTED ON KNOWING WHETHER HE WOULD PERMIT ME TO PURCHASE MYSELF AND OUR SON, HE TURNED TO ME IN A PETULANT MANNER, THRUST HIS HAND INTO HIS POCKET, DREW FORTH A BRIGHT SILVER QUARTER OF A DOLLAR, AND PROFFERING IT TO ME SAID:

LIZZIE, I HAVE TOLD YOU OFTEN NOT TO TROUBLE ME WITH SUCH A QUESTION. IF YOU REALLY WISH TO LEAVE ME, TAKE THIS QUARTER: IT WILL PAY THE PASSAGE OF YOURSELF AND THE BOY ON THE FERRY-BOAT, AND WHEN YOU ARE ON THE OTHER SIDE OF THE RIVER YOU WILL BE FREE."

Elizabeth Keckley
(an emancipated slavewoman's memoirs)
Behind The Scenes or Thirty Years a Slave and Four Years in the White House

Chapter VII
Woman, Create Wealth!

The classic best selling self-help book by Norman Cousins tells us to think and grow rich. The author reminds us that our very thoughts can help motivate our actions to allow extraordinary riches into our lives. Once the excitement of this and other books and seminars that spout off the same exaggerations is that most of us know there is much, much, more to getting rich than this. The fact is, ***everyone is not going to get rich simply by having the "right" thoughts*** and we all know it!

Moreover, most of us are not willing to pay the high price associated with making enormous amounts of money. For many that start their pursuits without the benefit of family money or extensive venture capital, they will find that the road to riches is paved with enormous sacrifices. These may include childlessness, poor eating and physical fitness habits, little time for hobbies and fun-filled activities, or little or no time for meaningful adult relationships such as friends or spouses. In addition, we all know you can roll the dice, take the gamble, and make all these sacrifices and still end up short of the mark due to circumstances primarily out of our control such as ill health, a lack luster economy, competition, embezzlement, and fraud.

And yet, most people regardless of race, gender, class, and even education levels, can aspire and attain a politically active, middle to lower upper-class, prosperous lifestyle filled with children, healthful eating and physical fitness habits, meaningful adult relationships, time for sailing, biking, traveling, volunteering, and more. Most of us can realistically achieve a life of independence, wealth, and power through successful entrepreneurship.

Think And Grow Prosperous

All of us will make a million dollars and have the opportunity to exercise a few basic financial guidelines to become financially independent. Where will these million dollars come from? You and your spouse will most likely earn **more** than a million bucks from your respective professions! The average income for an American family is now well over $25,000 per year. Even without a single raise, this means the average American family will earn over a forty-year span – much, much more than one million dollars. But as A. L. Williams, business tycoon and author of the pamphlet, "Common Sense" explains, "It is not how much money you earn, it's how much money you keep".

Most people live at or above their means. Most of us succumb to short term pleasures in lieu of long-term rewards. The terms waiting and saving have almost no meaning today. And yet waiting and saving are exactly what will make you prosperous and allow you to accumulate wealth.

The key word is "accumulate". It takes time along with a plan to successfully accumulate the assets you desire. While there are volumes written on how to manage and invest money, there are few common sense guides for the average American to ascribe to. Herein lies my contribution to the basics of how to think and grow prosperous. Since we are all going to make (at least) a million bucks, let's figure out what to do with it.

Guidelines For Building Wealth For Financial Independence

• Become an entrepreneur. When you become an independent small business owner, you can write off most expenditures thereby improve your standard of living while increasing the amount of cash you can legally preserve tax deferred (See Chapter VIII and your tax accountant or financial planner for details).

• Save a percentage of your income every month. This one is easier said than done. For some strange reason, we find it easier to commit to make car payments to a stranger than to commit money to our future, our children's futures, and ourselves.

• Pay yourself first with an automatic deposit into a tax deferred and invested savings program. This is a straightforward way to accumulate wealth. The more time you have, the better this plan will work for you. For example, if you set aside just $100 per month at 5% compounded interest for forty years, you will accumulate $148,856. If your average compounded interest rate is 10%, you will nearly quadruple your accumulated wealth and have $559, 650. This means that you could live a modest lifestyle drawing off only the interest so that your principal will last essentially forever. You could literally begin the start of your family's dynasty by leaving your offspring a substantial inheritance for them to use to launch their businesses.

Thus, any young American woman can become financially independent by retirement age by saving a mere $100 per month. For most of us, this means the difference between driving a new car and a used car. This is not much of a sacrifice when you consider the positive outcome down the road.

• Educate yourself on investment vehicles (especially IRA's, KEOGH's, mutual funds, DRIP's, and real estate). This probably became apparent in my earlier examples, which depicted the accumulated wealth difference between 5% and 10% compounded interest. Simply put, the higher the interest rate, the greater the return. In addition, the higher the interest rate the greater the risk. Commonsense must prevail here. I have successfully used the one-third, one-third, one-third rule recommended by many financial planners. One third of our invested savings are in lower (safer) interest rate vehicles; one third is in moderate interest rate vehicles; and the final third is in the highest interest rate vehicles.

• Acquaint yourself with what banks and other financial professionals call the rule of "72" which is: Your money will double at an exact point by dividing 72 by the percent interest. For example:

72	divided by	3% interest =	24 years
72	divided by	6% interest =	12 years
72	divided by	9% interest =	8 years
72	divided by	12% interest =	6 years

When you study this simple set of numbers, you will appreciate how important it is to rarely, if ever rely on certificates of deposits, bank savings accounts, and the like for any monies you hope to accumulate for retirement. Financial independence in your lifetime depends on getting modest to high levels of return on your money which can typically be achieved through mutual funds, DRIP's (Dividend Reinvestment Programs), and wisely chosen diverse groups of stocks. I found valuable insights into these investment vehicles and other practical wealth building ideas in the following publications:

"Common Sense" (Pamphlet), A.L. Williams, Parklake Publishers, Inc., Atlanta, GA, 1983.

"A Common Sense Guide To Personal Money Management" (Pamphlet), Staff Writers for American Express Financial Advisors Inc., Minneapolis, Minnesota, 1996.

Buying Stocks Without A Broker, The Best Selling Guide That Has Started Thousands of Investors on the Road To Commission-Free Investing, 2nd Edition, Charles B. Carlson, CFA, McGraw-Hill, New York, NY, 1992.

Bogle On Mutual Funds, New Perspectives for the Intelligent Investor, John C. Bogle, Dell Publishing, New York, NY, 1994.

Financial Self-Defense -- How To Win the Fight for Financial Freedom, Charles J. Givens, Simon and Schuster, New York, NY, 1990.

• Never finance a depreciating asset; and conversely, only finance appreciating assets. I found these simple guidelines made a significant difference in my life. For example, most people finance a new car loan. This is unwise because the asset you are financing is going down in value so quickly, that if you had to sell it the day after you bought it, you would take a 20% loss! So your $25,000 new car will loose $5,000 in value in just twenty-four hours. If your car has options, it will typically loose another 38% after twenty-four months. These are real dollars and it is your money. Moreover, when you add the interest charges on a four or five year car loan, you will pay six to eight thousand dollars in interest charges over the life of the loan. There is a better way.

Charles Givens, best selling author of Financial Self-defense, among others, encourages those of us who wish to preserve our hard earned money to, "Buy the car of your dreams, but only after it is two to two and a half years old". This way you can get the vehicle at sometimes half the original "new" sales price and with a little shopping around, you can get "like-new" cars. You can take the difference in the new-car payment and the used-car payment and put it into your tax deferred, invested savings program. And as mentioned earlier, for any twenty five-year-old, this one simple guideline applied for forty years can make you financially independent.

When you finance an appreciating asset, you are at least going to reap the benefits of an asset being valued higher than when you originally acquired it which helps to offset interest charges paid over the life of the loan. One example is real estate. While there are volumes written on this subject which can get quite complicated, I wish to stress only the basic advantages of owner occupied home ownership.

Home ownership, for starters, is still one of the best ways for the average American woman to accumulate wealth using time and common sense. I can remember my own hesitancy in taking the plunge. As a recent college graduate in 1976, I was single and earning a reasonable income and renting a very nice apartment for $325 per month. I had all the "right reasons" for not buying a home: single, wanted to remain flexible on where I chose to live, no down payment money, frightened of a 30 year mortgage/commitment, should wait until I got married, etc.

I had the good fortune to meet my future husband who encouraged me to talk to a savvy Realtor. The Realtor showed me how I could connect with a motivated seller who was willing to carry back a second mortgage and I could become a homeowner immediately. Moreover, while the mortgage payments on the small home I ultimately purchased were 30% higher than my rental payments, my cash position remained the same because I could legally increase my deductions which provided the difference in more net income in every paycheck.

Now, here is the punch line; because I had used common sense on the home I purchased, I acquired a place that was appreciating in value. When I sold it four years later, I made a gross profit of over $40,000. This was real money; a check was made out to me, Zella Jackson. At that time, this was the largest lump sum of money I had ever received -- and I was not yet thirty years old.

Now, real life unfolded in the meantime; I got married a year and a half after I bought the home and therefore had to rent it out until I sold it three and a half years later. I even relocated to another area! But this and other subsequent real estate investments I have made make the wisdom of home ownership for the accumulation of wealth – abundantly clear.

Another scenario I wish to share is a typical long-term financial planning strategy that works for most people. Buy a single family home (townhouses and condominiums don't tend to be as good of an investment) as your primary residence in an area that your research shows will more than likely appreciate over a ten to thirty year period. Look for areas that are experiencing growth (Developers look ten to thirty years out to buy the land they intend to build track houses on in the future; by buying that far in advance, they are assured of making substantial profits down the road). Anticipate a two to three year window of opportunity to sell at a peak price. Single family real estate values tend to fluctuate but if you look at the longer term, the fluctuations continue to climb upwards.

In addition, you will want to time your "window of opportunity" after you reach the age of fifty-five. The current laws still exempt you from paying taxes on the first $125,000 of profit from the sale of your primary residence if you are over fifty-five. You can integrate whatever the actual gain you achieve into your plans.

Once your home reaches a peak value within your pre-determined window of opportunity, sell it! Don't hang on for more profit. It may well be poised for a drop and you will need to extend your time frame beyond what is comfortable for you thereby minimizing your gains.

Once you sell your home at its peak, after the age of fifty-five, your options are many. You may wish to pay cash for a townhouse or condominium if your children are grown up. Or you may wish to put an infusion of cash into your tax deferred invested savings program which will provide the opportunity for significant gains.

Now, when you do this as part of an overall wealth building strategy, you will have additional cash that is difficult to match and accumulate from merely saving. And the best part is that you can maintain the same lifestyle (if not improve it) as a homeowner vs. a renter while building wealth for your future. After all, we all want to have a roof over our heads and the very same money you would give to a landlord can be given to a bank (to pay off your mortgage) which allows you to accumulate substantial wealth.

• Support only legislators who support small business and reduce taxes for the working class. The final chapter of this book reminds us of how important our individual votes are but I wish to stress the point here as well. Keep your eyes open for those politicians who are slowly but surely taking away our ability to achieve financial independence. When the time comes, vote them out of office. Similarly, vote those new candidates into office that promise to protect our legacy to achieve the American Dream of financial independence. While this dream is still alive, it is clearly in jeopardy.

• Get started now and put time on your side. The more time you give yourself to work your plan, the greater the likelihood of achieving financial independence. Take a close look at the following chart. It really drives home the importance of starting early and being consistent with your wealth accumulation program.

THE MAGIC OF COMPOUND INTEREST

The figures below illustrate how an investment of $100 each month would perform at 11% for a person who begins investing at age 30 and stops 7 years later (Investor A). They compare with a person who waits till age 38 to begin saving the same amount and continues to age 65 (Investor B).

	Investor A		Investor B	
Age	Annual Investment	Acct. Value	Annual Investment	Acct. Value
31	$1,200	$1,262	$0	$0
32	$1,200	$2,671	$0	$0
33	$1,200	$4,242	$0	$0
34	$1,200	$5,996	$0	$0
35	$1,200	$7,952	$0	$0
36	$1,200	$10,134	$0	$0
37	$1,200	$12,569	$0	$0
38	$0	$14,023	$1,200	$1,262
39	$0	$15,646	$1,200	$2,671
40	$0	$17,457	$1,200	$4,242
41	$0	$19,477	$1,200	$5,996
42	$0	$21,731	$1,200	$7,952
43	$0	$24,245	$1,200	$10,135
44	$0	$27,051	$1,200	$12,569
45	$0	$30,181	$1,200	$15,286
46	$0	$33,674	$1,200	$18,318
47	$0	$37,570	$1,200	$21,700
48	$0	$41,918	$1,200	$25,473
49	$0	$46,769	$1,200	$29,683
50	$0	$52,181	$1,200	$34,381
51	$0	$58,219	$1,200	$39,622
52	$0	$64,956	$1,200	$45,469
53	$0	$72,473	$1,200	$51,993
54	$0	$80,860	$1,200	$59,272
55	$0	$90,217	$1,200	$67,393
56	$0	$100,656	$1,200	$76,454
57	$0	$112,304	$1,200	$86,564
58	$0	$125,300	$1,200	$97,843
59	$0	$139,799	$1,200	$110,428
60	$0	$155,977	$1,200	$124,469
61	$0	$174,549	$1,200	$140,135
62	$0	$194,165	$1,200	$157,613
63	$0	$216,633	$1,200	$177,115
64	$0	$241,701	$1,200	$198,872
65	$0	$269,671	$1,200	$223,148
Total Invested at Age 65:		**$8,400**		**$33,600**
Account Value at Age 65:		**$269,671**		**$223,148**

- <u>Many financial planners also recommend diversification as a key element of your success. Here's why:</u>

The chart below compares $25,000 invested at a fixed 8% for 25 years vs. divided among five different investments with returns on each portion varying from becoming worthless to a 15% return.

Investment:	$25,000			$25,000
Fixed 8%		$5,000	becomes worthless	0
		$5,000	earns 0%	$5,000
		$5,000	earns 5%	$16,931
		$5,000	earns 10%	$54,174
		$5,000	earns 15%	$164,595
Future Value:	**$171,212**			**$257,631**

• Finally, take a look at how long your money will last once you have accumulated your retirement fund. Again, the size of the withdrawals and the rate of return on your investments can make an enormous impact on the longevity of your portfolio.

HOW LONG WILL YOUR MONEY LAST?

Here's how long you can expect your savings to last, making the following monthly withdrawals.

Starting with	10 yrs	20 yrs	Forever (withdrawing interest only)
$50,000	$535	$337	$222
$100,000	$1,069	$674	$443
$150,000	$1,604	$1,011	$665
$200,000	$2,138	$1,349	$886
$250,000	$2,673	$1,686	$1,108
$500,000	$5,345	$3,372	$2,216
$750,000	$8,025	$5,055	$3,330

Based on 5.5% annual yield, compounded quarterly. Investment performance can dramatically affect these numbers. Inflation can also seriously affect the value of the withdrawals.

Chart derived from "A Common Sense Guide to Personal Money Management", staff writers for American Express Financial Advisors Inc.

One Plan To Achieve Financial Independence

The following plan, while oversimplified, can provide you the kind of example you may need to get your own plan committed to paper. Also, refer back to pages 54, 55, and 56 as you begin your journey to financial independence.

1) Use The Active Voice & Be Specific: In 2036, I have $500,000 and while 10% interest is possible, I plan conservatively for 5.5% and draw a modest $2,216 per month forever which leaves my $500,000 intact and provide an inheritance for my offspring (See How Long Will Your Money Last?, previous page).

2) Specify Your Wealth Accumulation Plan: In 1996, I am 25 years old and I put $100 per month into my tax deferred invested savings program of mutual funds whereby an average yield of 10% compounded interest accumulates to over $500,000 by 2036 (two pages back).

For those with less time now, but who were fortunate enough to have acquired a home and built up substantial equity. In addition, this "person" chose entrepreneurship whereby saving $1,000 is entirely workable, the following short plan is offered.

1) Use The Active Voice & Be Specific: In 2006, I have $500,000 and while 10% interest is possible, I plan conservatively for 5.5% and draw a modest $2,216 per month forever which leaves my $500,000 intact and provide an inheritance for my offspring (See How Long Will Your Money Last?, previous page).

2) Specify Your Wealth Accumulation Plan: In 1996, I am 55 years old and I put $1000 per month into my tax deferred invested savings program of mutual funds whereby an average yield of 10% compounded interest accumulates to over $200,000 by 2006 (see page 69). I liquidate my primary residence which I have resided in for twenty years with a profit of $250,000 and add that to my $200,000 accumulation. I sell my business to my adult children for $100,000 (which they finance) and add that to the other two sums for $500,000 total accumulated wealth. I pay cash for $50,000 for a pre-fab home on one acre of land (in rural, low priced America) that I purchased, in cash, ten years ago (1996).

Recognize, each of these scenarios is relatively conservative and do not include any social security benefits that you may be entitled to (although the future of that program is in question). For those who are more aggressive, more substantial wealth accumulation is not only possible, but also probable. See your financial planner today and get going because time is a wasting.

Let me conclude this chapter with one final thought. The phrase, "financial planning" is an unfortunate misnomer. In contrast, "**wealth building accumulation plan**" is more proactive and gets to the heart of the matter. Remember to simplify, focus, and execute beginning right now!

Chapter VIII
Woman, Build A Business!

Webster defines power as the possession of control, authority, or influence over others. Indeed, the dual concepts of a woman with power seem almost contradictory. So much so that when I talk to women who, in fact, are powerful (successful business owners, top level executives, and the like) -- they have difficulty describing themselves in these terms.

It is time we get comfortable with obtaining and exercising power and that begins with first gaining possession of control over ourselves. And when we control our own productivity, we control our opportunities to produce wealth.

What follows is the road map for any woman who chooses to set herself free by virtue of providing a product or service to other businesses. It is exactly how I have successfully run my own consulting and wholesaling businesses over the years. Once you discover the business you were meant to be in, the only limitation to the amount of wealth you create is between you, your family, and God.

One Family's Journey To Purpose

There are numerous books on discovering one's calling, however, I have found that most people already "know" what their calling is but simply refuse to listen to their own hearts. As a consultant, I often visit this topic with my clients even though most of them have already invested considerable resources toward a particular endeavor. Invariably, the answer lies with the yearnings from our youth or an "unthinkable vision" that thrusts itself into our dreams as we journey through one of life's passages or turning points. I encourage you to listen to your own heart.

In the summer of 1981, I had the opportunity to meet a "temporarily lost" couple in their thirties on the lovely island of Maui. The husband, Gary, was a trained pharmacist, and the wife, Andrea, was a schoolteacher. Neither was practicing their respective professions, however, when we met. They were attending to one of life's passages and contemplating the next stage of their lives. They had recently relocated from Detroit, Michigan to escape the high crime and extraordinary pressures of operating a seven-day a week drugs store.

I met Gary in a sales seminar that I was conducting for his employer. I discussed the mechanics of selling effectively but more importantly for him, I discussed the significance of discovering ones purpose in life. I gave numerous "real-life" examples, then referenced studies and experts to underscore the point that a person would only find true happiness and the epitome of success upon discovering ones purpose. This, in conjunction with properly written long and short-term goals would empower a person to their highest level of achievement.

Gary went home and shared all of this with his wife and they awakened in themselves a nearly dead dream of Andrea being a famous artist, and he being her promoter. Andrea's dream was so "unthinkable" that she had primarily painted for herself and close family members. In fact, she had hidden what later proved to be some of her best works, in the closet!

Well, the ending to this story is quite remarkable. This "temporarily lost" couple ended up spending the last sixteen years building a successful art wholesaling and publishing business while developing Andrea's reputation to world-wide collectible status. Gary and Andrea have created enviable wealth while raising their children in a nurturing family business environment.

So, go ahead -- listen to <u>your</u> dreams. The answer is beating in step with the rhythm of your own heart. And even if the answer leads you down an unorthodox path, know that this is the path for you.

Imagine for a moment the reaction of Andrea's friends and relatives upon sharing her vision of becoming an internationally renowned artist selling original artworks for over twenty thousand dollars and being a creative catalyst for world peace. Imagine yet again, Andrea's pervasive sense of empowerment upon choosing to step in concert with ones purpose. Finally, imagine Andrea's sense of achievement upon realizing her dreams.

Marry Talent With Business Concept

One key to Andrea and Gary's success is they married their talents with a business concept. Andrea was (and still is) a talented watercolorist painter and Gary was (and still is) a super-salesperson/promoter. Together they made an unstoppable combination.

Similarly, you have talents that lend themselves to a business concept. You also have probably spent many years in a particular profession that may exercise some of your talents. My former bookkeeper, Jackie, had a lifelong talent with numbers. She worked for me as an employee for three years and then started (after twenty years of thinking about it) her own home-based bookkeeping firm. One of my husband's technical support employees, Tim, worked for him for two years supporting software installations and then went out on his own with a computer literacy and training business. A soft-spoken yet assertive person, he had learned that he was particularly good at walking people through their software programs even when there were snafus.

A good friend of ours, Talonna, noted she had a gift for teaching. She has a non-profit institute that she runs from home and has done everything from computer literacy training to producing and distributing hurricane preparedness videos.

The woman who directed my video-training program runs her business from her home. Karen does freelance work in the broad category we call the film industry. She assembled a team consisting of a cameraperson, makeup artist, lighting expert, etc. to construct a set and shoot my program. Karen did all of the editing, the lead-in, and cut-ins herself, plus brought the $10,000 project in within budget and on time. She had learned as a young girl that she "loved" the performing arts and especially film. Moreover, she knew how to work with performers to help them be their best on film. My list of examples could fill an entire book. The bottom-line is I am confident the best way for you to discover your purpose is to make note of your talents, then build your business concept around it.

For clarity, I have decided to focus on two types of home-based businesses to illustrate how any woman can create wealth through entrepreneurship: (1) an art wholesaling business, and (2) a consulting firm. Both are based on my own firms whereby I have direct experience with success for all of the recommendations provided. In both cases, I limit my comments to selling products and/or services to businesses because I feel that there are many overlooked opportunities for those small business owners wishing to develop business accounts. These often-missed opportunities include: (1) available market share, (2) life-long repeat business, (3) large average invoice amounts, (4) Monday through Friday work schedule to choose within, (5) regular payment schedules, and much more.

Real-life Examples:

(1) A Products Business -The Fine Art Network, and (2) A Services Business -Novasearch Consultants

My comments that follow reflect my direct experience with two types of home-based businesses. One business sells products and the other sells time (services). I trust these two simplified examples will prove to be solid benchmarks for you to make decisions concerning your own venture.

Getting Started

How exactly does one create wealth by providing products and services to businesses? I chose to develop a company that provided contemporary fine art to small businesses as my focus. I had developed expertise in this area and felt confident in my merchandising decisions, marketing strategies, business plan and execution. This was the "marry talent with business concept" step.

Then I asked myself, "How can I - a small art business owner - sell products or services to other (mostly) small business owners who are very much like myself?" When I thought of this endeavor in these terms, somehow the whole process seemed like a natural extension of my purpose.

This section expands on how **you** can approach the very important small business market with products and services you have expertise in. Doing business with other small businesses has many benefits you will want to consider.

First, it is a rather uncrowded market place for most parts of the country. The challenges lie in setting up an appropriate price structure, sub-contracts, scheduling appointment time for making presentations, designing and assembling easy to understand yet professionally polished visuals (as in a portfolio), allowing for what can be lengthy lead times prior to receiving deposits, and efficiently expanding into more accounts. These challenges as well as many others, will be discussed in the following section so that you can begin to set up (or strengthen) an existing small business.

Define Your Role. There are numerous roles you may elect to play in developing your client base. Do you wish to simply represent a product line or will you provide support services, as well? Some product representatives will lend, trade, buy back, and offer many peripheral services that business accounts appreciate. Will you assist the business owner (or his/her facilities manager) with making leasing arrangements? Recognize that some of these services can become quite daunting for your larger accounts. The services you "advertise" and will need to provide for a close-in deadline can be a bit of a logistics shock for the small business owner. And yet, how you handle such a situation can be pivotal in whether you will have the opportunity to make such a sale ever again in your immediate region (remember, good and bad news always travels fast).

It is important, then, for you to define what roles you will play ahead of time so that most contingencies can be worked out before problems arise. For example, if you decide to sell art to businesses and wish to install large quantities of framed prints, find another small business owner who is already equipped with vans, etc., so that you can quickly sub-contract any jobs that are too large for you to easily handle. But work out the details ahead of time and have the terms, conditions, and liabilities all in writing.

Determine The Best Products And/Or Service You Wish To Provide. When supplying products, research the specific brands that you anticipate providing to your clientele. Determine the strength of the companies you plan to represent. Check their references, talk to other distributors, and ensure yourself the time, terms, and potential payback is worth all of your efforts.

For example, when I contemplated providing art to businesses, I had to research the artists and their respective publishers. Some of the questions I answered for myself when I started an art wholesaling business (The Fine Art Network) included:

- "Are delivery times reliable?"
- "What do I do in case of a return; how much of my money is at risk?"
- "As a small distributor, can I get competitive wholesale pricing?"
- "What is the turn around time from order placement to order received?"
- "How salable is this artist and imagery in the region I serve?"
- "Can I request and do justice to an exclusive contract?"

As you can see, the industry you choose will dictate the questions you must answer. In general, you want to provide a unique product on an exclusive basis in your region at the lowest possible price. The closer you come to this ideal, the better your likelihood of success (assuming there is a demand for what you offer).

Many of the same principles for products apply to services. The key caveat centers on duplication. If you decide to offer a specialty service that is personality related, recognize that if you are ill, there is no one who can stand-in for you which can provide some limitations.

For example, in my consulting practice, I am "The Art of Selling Art" lady -- period. No substitute will do. So I have had to plan around this. This means, for example, that my fees must be high. This high fee structure is justified in part due to my reputation but also because there are only so many trips per year I intend to make due to my family priorities. This relatively limited travel schedule, in turn, creates an instant high demand and ""une voila"" -- I earn two to three times the amount in half the time. Another example of this consideration is that I must schedule myself responsibly so as to allow for some flexibility in the event of personal illness. And finally, to accommodate my smaller clients (who become my future larger clients!) I provide video instruction, public seminars, books, and phone consultations for a reasonable fee.

Identify Your Target Markets

What businesses do you wish to sell your products and/or services to? This may sound like a silly question but surely the computer literacy consultant who specializes in children grades K-6, then packages their verbal and collateral presentations around this specialty has a much greater chance of getting a particular private school project than the generalist. Your credibility in the beginning might be due to the fact that you installed such a program as an employee for XYZ Corporation or ABC School and thereby make you well suited for the project. Once you land a few projects, your credibility will lie in your experience and good reputation. Some target markets to consider if you are a home-based entrepreneur who reps anything from art to bookkeeping services include:

- Professional Offices including the offices of doctors, attorneys, CPA's

- Model Homes
- Restaurants
- Developers
- Manufacturing facilities
- Sales offices
- Hospitals
- High-end property management firms
- Hotels
- Research facilities
- Universities

If you wish to be a generalist then you should construct your collateral material so that you can appear to be a specialist when you make your presentations to any specific target market. Sometimes the region you serve may be sufficiently small so as to dictate remaining a generalist particularly if you wish to minimize travel. On the other hand, I know several small business owners who are willing to travel long distances and find that having built a reputation in one specialty allows them to sell effectively throughout the entire country.

Use Trade Shows and Trade Journals To Fine Tune Your Plans

Once you have narrowed down your industry but are still deciding on the details of what to offer, bypass the bookstores and libraries and go straight to a major trade show. The insights you will gain from this experience will prove invaluable.

First of all, a major trade show (which you may very well have to travel long distance to) is up to the minute. It is happening, literally right now. Anything in a book is at least six (and more likely) eighteen months old. You need to know the latest, up to the minute information before you make a considerable commitment to the details of your business plan.

Imagine for a moment, that as a new business owner in a potentially new field, what it would be like to chat with your competition; peruse top level collateral material (that you can model); attend "free" informational seminars from experts; and qualify potential suppliers? And, perhaps most important, be able to do all of this in a matter of a weekend. Well, welcome to your industry's top trade show for the year.

I started my independent small business career as a generalist consultant in the following areas: marketing, management, and sales. I was considering specializing in one of two industries, art and banking. While each was totally different, the one thing they had in common was I had a solid track record with both categories of clients. Well, my first sojourn took me eight thousand miles from home (Honolulu to New York City) to what was billed as the largest art trade show in the world. The time I spent there and the insights I gained were essential and proved pivotal in my career.

Similarly, I perused the trade journals (which are often provided free at the trade shows) which added even more useful data. For example, at a glance I was able to determine with some accuracy, who were the largest and potentially best qualified prospects for my services: those with large full-page, professionally done ads, press releases, articles, etc. No over the counter book or library reference can give you the same "real-time" information about a specific industry as when you attend a trade show and study current trade journals.

Develop Your Business Plan

The business plan is as critical to your success as your own personal set of long and short range goals. The business plan, however, focuses on just those elements that influence your firm. One book I have found very helpful is, The Entrepreneur's Master Planning Guide -- How To Launch A Successful Business, by Welsh and White. The following should be thoroughly thought out, then concisely summarized:

- Business Concept
- Background
- Equipment Needs
- Marketing Overview
    - Target Market Defined
    - Promotion Campaign
    - Advertising or PR Schedule (if appropriate)
    - List of Competition
    - Human Resources Available

- Financial Performance
    - Projected Income Statements (1st and 2nd Year)
    - Projected Balance Sheet
    - Budgeted Monthly Income Statement Notes

Projected Cash Flow Statements

I put this together for my consulting business at a time when my husband and I were considering getting jobs! We were surviving from one meager consulting project to another. As described earlier, we first, we re-connected with our purpose, short and long range personal goals, and then we examined how we could revitalize our failing consulting business. Here is an example of the elements listed above based on the actual plan I devised for ourselves. While the numbers have been changed and some detail has been simplified for clarity, I feel this example can be used as a model for anyone starting a small home-based business.

NOVASEARCH CONSULTANTS

Business Plan for a High Quality Service Business

Prepared by

Zella N. Jackson

Business Concept

Novasearch Consultants provides Business Development Consulting services to clients specializing in "high-ticket" luxury items/services who wish to increase sales, profitability, and productivity. Novasearch obtains outstanding results through specialization, innovative approaches, integrity, and hard work.

Location of Operations

Novasearch Consultants is located at 1164 Bishop Street, Honolulu, Hawaii. We cultivate clients throughout the state of Hawaii and conduct business on the islands of Oahu, Maui, Kauai, and Hawaii.

Services

<u>Business Development Consulting Services</u>

Novasearch Consultants specializes in Business Development Services for Art Galleries, Fine Jewelry Retailers and Marketers of Antiques and Fine Collectibles. Novasearch has developed training programs specially designed and customized to fit each client's needs. These sessions build effective sales presentation skills, product knowledge, and self-management techniques for sales consultants and sales management personnel. These sessions become an integral part of sales meetings, brainstorming sessions, and strategically timed training sessions.

Training manuals, incentive programs, attitude surveys, audio and video training/assessment are among the aids used to develop appropriate learning systems.

A full product line has also been developed including a published book, videos, organizers, personnel manuals, a newsletter, and software.

Market Considerations

Throughout the United States, the world of fine art, antiques, and designer jewelry has seen dramatic growth within the past five years with the expansion of fine collectible appreciation by a diverse and energetic new public. This provides opportunities for Business

Consultants like Novasearch, because these retailers require intermittent specialty advice versus full time. Examples:

> As a business grows and matures, the owners find themselves wishing to delegate routine but important matters to employees. Without clear-cut procedures written down for easy access, confusion and mistakes are unavoidable. An expert procedure writer would be required to do an appropriate, efficient job, but such expertise is impractical for a small business full-time.
>
> Basic sales training is essential for any business but a full-time sales trainer would be impractical for most small businesses.
>
> A well-trained marketing expert would be required to project important industry trends and recommend well-structured promotions and advertising campaigns. This expertise is too expensive on a full-time, in-house basis.

Novasearch Consultants provides such services on an "as needed" basis for clients throughout the state. Further, advances in microcomputers, software, and learning systems have made it affordable for small to medium sized companies to incorporate the latest technologies. This has made many small as well as large business owners to view business management consultants as fundamental to the success of their businesses as their CPAs.

Novasearch Consultants is dedicated toward the highest quality Business Development products and services. Novasearch is committed to practical, ethical and professional work and "gets results".

Resume of Owner
Zella Jackson

A Business and Sales Development expert with a B.S. degree in Mechanical Engineering and an M.B.A. Operations Management from Michigan State University. Extensive experience in Sales and Marketing, Operations Management, and Sales Staff Management.

Formerly, IBM's General Products Division Systems Operations Manager with multi-million dollar budget responsibility: coordinated projects that affected over one thousand people.

Also, a former Marketing Specialist for Dow Chemical Company; headed a successful national marketing campaign to commercialize newly introduced reverse osmosis membrane modules.

As a Business Development Consultant with Novasearch Consultants, she has orchestrated sales increases 30% to 200% within six to eighteen months for client organizations such as C.S. Wo, First Hawaiian Bank, Kapalua Bay Hotel, von Maritime Inc., and Dolphin Galleries. Innovative training methods, creative-marketing strategies, effective sales staff development techniques, and insightful management development methods are used to obtain results while achieving profitability objectives and improving overall morale.

Known throughout the state as a featured lecturer and guest speaker. Featured in educational films and publications. Selected in 1982 the State of Hawaii Career Woman of the Year.

Marketing Plan --Novasearch Products

Products include: Public Sales Training Seminars ($395), The Complete Personnel Manual -- A Guide For Retailers To Create A Customized Policies and Procedures Manual ($100), The Newsletter ($29.00), and the video entitled, "The Art of Selling To The Japanese".

Marketing Approach: Combination of direct mail and phone follow-up, as well as distribution of literature at two major trade shows each year.

A total of five direct mail campaigns have been scheduled this year (one bulk; four 1st class).

Each 1st class mailing of 500 will be followed up with phone calls.

The two trade shows offer retail-like selling opportunities as well as PR opportunities. Contacted the show promoters to request a speaking slot.

Implementation: 2,350 1st class brochures/letters and 6,000 bulk rate brochures/letters will be sent to targeted retailers coast to coast as well as in Hawaii.

Bulk mailings will be sent out through local mailing service; 1st class mailings to be hand-addressed in-house to assure maximum attention. Approximately 1100 prospects receiving 1st class mailings will be contacted by phone.

Goals: The Novasearch Sales Training Program to be known as "The Number One" program for those specializing in high-ticket merchandise throughout the country.

A minimum of 15 paid in full participants at each public seminar; with $1,500 in material sales in conjunction with each program.

An additional $2,000 per mailing is projected for gross receipts as straight mail order.

A total of $50,000 in gross receipts is conservatively projected. Sell $20,000 in products at each trade show.

Marketing Plan -- Novasearch Consulting Services

Services include:	Customized, in-house sales and management training and consultations with owners/managers of primarily high-end retailers in Hawaii. Contracts of six to twelve months' duration will provide the main gross receipts from services rendered.
Approach:	Renewals and referrals are the primary ways Novasearch will achieve sales projections on services.
Goals:	$50,000 in gross receipts will be obtained through this retainer program. Breakdown: One large ($1,500), one medium ($1,000), and four small ($500) retainers will be managed for the year.

PROJECTED FINANCIAL PERFORMANCE

for

Novasearch Consultants

Zella Jackson

DESCRIPTION	Jan-96	Feb-96	Mar-96	Apr-96	May-96
SUMMARY					
INCOME	$7,800	$7,800	$11,500	$7,800	$7,800
COST OF GOODS SOLD	$395	$395	$950	$2,095	$395
PAYROLL EXPENSES	$4,375	$4,375	$4,375	$4,375	$4,375
SALES EXPENSES	$150	$150	$150	$150	$150
OCCUPANCY EXPENSES	$840	$840	$840	$820	$820
G&A EXPENSES	$1,174	$1,224	$1,470	$1,474	$1,174
NET OPER. BEFORE TAX	$866	$816	$3,715	($1,114)	$886
YTD NET PBT	$866	$1,682	$5,397	$4,283	$5,169
INCOME					
Consulting	$6,500	$6,500	$6,500	$6,500	$6,500
Books, Tapes, Etc.	$1,300	$1,300	$5,000	$1,300	$1,300
COST OF GOODS SOLD					
Books, Tapes, Etc.	$195	$195	$750	$195	$195
Direct Travel Expenses	$200	$200	$200	$1,900	$200
EXPENSES					
PAYROLL EXPENSES					
Owner's Salary	$4,000	$4,000	$4,000	$4,000	$4,000
Health Plan	$375	$375	$375	$375	$375
SALES EXPENSES					
Advertising	$150	$150	$150	$150	$150
Merchant Dscnt. Fees					
OCCUPANCY EXPENSES					
Home office depreciation	$700	$700	$700	$700	$700
Utilities	$65	$65	$65	$45	$45
Maintenance	$50	$50	$50	$50	$50
Insurance, Furn. & Equip.	$25	$25	$25	$25	$25
G&A EXPENSES					
Accounting Fees	$100	$100	$100	$400	$100
Contributions	$50	$50	$50	$50	$50
Dues & Subscriptions	$20	$20	$20	$20	$20
Entertainment		$50			
Freight In/Out	$15	$15	$15	$15	$15
Insurance, Liab. & Comp.	$125	$125	$125	$125	$125
Legal Fees	$50	$50	$50	$50	$50
Misc. Printed Materials	$25	$25	$25	$25	$25
Miscellaneous	$50	$50	$50	$50	$50
Outside Services	$50	$50	$50	$50	$50
Permits, Fees, etc.	$25	$25	$25	$25	$25
Postage	$45	$45	$45	$45	$45
Repair & Maint.	$50	$50	$50	$50	$50
Sales Taxes	$104	$104	$400	$104	$104
Supplies, General	$40	$40	$40	$40	$40
Telephone	$275	$275	$275	$275	$275
Travel	$150	$150	$150	$150	$150

Jun-96	Jul-96	Aug-96	Sep-96	Oct-96	Nov-96	Dec-96	Total
$7,800	$7,800	$7,800	$7,800	$13,500	$7,800	$7,800	$103,000
$395	$395	$395	$395	$3,850	$395	$395	$10,450
$4,375	$4,375	$4,375	$4,375	$4,375	$4,375	$4,375	$52,500
$150	$150	$150	$150	$150	$150	$150	$1,800
$820	$840	$840	$840	$820	$840	$840	$10,000
$1,174	$1,174	$1,174	$1,174	$1,630	$1,174	$1,174	$15,190
$886	$866	$866	$866	$2,675	$866	$866	$13,060
$6,055	$6,921	$7,787	$8,653	$11,328	$12,194	$13,060	13%
$6,500	$6,500	$6,500	$6,500	$6,500	$6,500	$6,500	$78,000
$1,300	$1,300	$1,300	$1,300	$7,000	$1,300	$1,300	$25,000
$195	$195	$195	$195	$1,050	$195	$195	$3,750
$200	$200	$200	$200	$2,800	$200	$200	$6,700
$4,000	$4,000	$4,000	$4,000	$4,000	$4,000	$4,000	$48,000
$375	$375	$375	$375	$375	$375	$375	$4,500
$150	$150	$150	$150	$150	$150	$150	$1,800
							$0
$700	$700	$700	$700	$700	$700	$700	$8,400
$45	$65	$65	$65	$45	$65	$65	$700
$50	$50	$50	$50	$50	$50	$50	$600
$25	$25	$25	$25	$25	$25	$25	$300
$100	$100	$100	$100	$100	$100	$100	$1,500
$50	$50	$50	$50	$50	$50	$50	$600
$20	$20	$20	$20	$20	$20	$20	$240
							$50
$15	$15	$15	$15	$15	$15	$15	$180
$125	$125	$125	$125	$125	$125	$125	$1,500
$50	$50	$50	$50	$50	$50	$50	$600
$25	$25	$25	$25	$25	$25	$25	$300
$50	$50	$50	$50	$50	$50	$50	$600
$50	$50	$50	$50	$50	$50	$50	$600
$25	$25	$25	$25	$25	$25	$25	$300
$45	$45	$45	$45	$45	$45	$45	$540
$50	$50	$50	$50	$50	$50	$50	$600
$104	$104	$104	$104	$560	$104	$104	$2,000
$40	$40	$40	$40	$40	$40	$40	$480
$275	$275	$275	$275	$275	$275	$275	$3,300
$150	$150	$150	$150	$150	$150	$150	$1,800

Again, while the sample business plan provided is for a consulting business, I feel confident it will give you insights into how you may wish to construct your own small business plan regardless of its specific orientation. Happily, most women who are committed to such a plan can earn $45,000 plus per year (see Owner's Salary) after expenses. Moreover, many of the expenses pay for your lifestyle. I must offer two important footnotes to this financial projection "exercise":

(1) When you develop this paperwork for the first time, you will probably feel like you are pulling it "out of a hat". After all, if you have little or no track record as a small business owner, how can you anticipate your gross revenues? Well, barring major shifts in the market place, if you have, in fact, based your plan on the type of research that I described, you will find your projections will tend to be reasonably close -- if not startling close to your actual results.

(2) Once I put this paperwork together, I added some letters of appreciation, a list of clientele (however, meager up to that point), the previous years lackluster tax return, along with my company's flyers and brochures. I took the complete package to our bank and was successful in getting a substantial line of credit that provided important capital for my firm's next step.

Indeed, the belief in one's abilities to create wealth plays a significant role in one's ultimate success in doing so.

Once you have your business plan in place, it is just a matter of executing your plan. Now that you have "talked the talked", you must "walk the walk".

Determine Your Pricing

Now you have determined your vision, married talent with your business concept, obtained hard-cold and "real-time" data from trade shows/journals, selected your industry and target markets and now must fine-tune your business plan. Price structures will first be addressed as you flesh out your projected income and cash flow statements, however, I would like you to consider some specifics as you "play around with the numbers."

The pricing of products sold to businesses can be significantly different from standard retail pricing. Most small business owners that you will be presenting yourself to are well aware of trade discounts. The watchwords here are **always be competitive** if not priced less than your competitors. For example, a new filter company in Hawaii opened to compete with one other company who had enjoyed essentially a monopoly on providing replacement filters for office buildings' and industrial facilities' air cooling systems. The working partner in the firm, Min, decided the best way for her to get her piece of the market (at least in the beginning) was to offer the identical product for less. It worked. Remember, if it is your intent to sell products to businesses in any big way, you will need to begin to think of yourself as a wholesaler with lower margins and high volume. Those of you who have computerized spreadsheets to play around with can quickly see how a smaller percent margin for most price levels can add up dollar-wise when you interject large volumes.

Also, recognize that you may wish to cut your margin (the difference between your cost and the price you sell your product for) in order to get your first few projects. In some of these cases, just getting the project may require the slimmest of margins but the permanent "advertising" aspect of such a project would be priceless.

Set Your Goals

Once you know what roles you wish to play, have identified your target markets, and have established your pricing schema, then you can effectively set goals. In addition to the obvious dollar amounts you plan to sell, incorporate interim task oriented goals that will help ensure your success. For example, set a date for when your portfolio will be completed, business cards/stationary designed and printed, preliminary site visits completed of your intended target markets, and so on.

As always, write these goals down and monitor your progress on an on-going basis. Once all the preliminaries are in place, set goals for prospecting, time devoted to direct sales calls, and number of presentations made.

Prospecting

Many small business owners will begin prospecting for accounts from their initial circle of influence derived from acquaintances, business associates, and relatives. This can be an excellent way to get started. Go ahead and set up an appointment with any business owner (including those doctors, dentists, and attorneys you have been buying from all along). Once you have begun, a never-ending stream of referrals can be harvested from any initial circle of influence comprised of twenty or more qualified clients. Remember a satisfied client will give you an average of five qualified referrals. Recognize how getting yourself set up ahead of time can have a big influence on how successful you will be when you approach your initial "circle". It is one thing to tell a business owner, "I have been thinking of possibly getting into corporate art sales and I know you know the person in-charge of that hotel renovation project. Could you introduce me to him/her?" It is quite another to say instead, "I have invested this past six months researching what art best enhances hotel interiors. It was quite a challenge. And I thought the eight years experience I had in hotel management gave me sufficient insights. But once I got more into it, I learned all the nuances that allow art to convey a hotel's image and ambiance to its guests. (Dialogue) You know, it occurs to me that you rub shoulders with (name of individual); perhaps we could all have lunch down at the club".

Beginning with an initial circle of influence is great but what if you are brand new to your product and wish to sell to businesses far removed from those you already know? Someone wise once said you are no more than five people away from anyone you wish to meet. I certainly have found this to be true whenever I have gone after new markets. I refer to this as top down selling which is a particularly important distinction for a primarily direct sales endeavor. In other words, anytime your entire business is derived from making sales appointments (as would be the case for most home-based businesses), I recommend you decide who you wish to sell to and then find a way to meet those individuals.

I built my consulting practice from scratch using this approach. Further, I had recently relocated to a new state while simultaneously starting this new consulting business (something I would not recommend to anyone). One of the things I did was immediately join a few professional organizations that had business owners and key decision-makers of my targeted market as members. I, then, went to the local chamber of commerce and bought their directory. It so happens, the directory was arranged alphabetically by company name and each had a brief description of the company, its size, primary goals, address, phone number, and the owner's full name and photograph. I literally went through this directory and hand picked my first clients. Of course, closing ratios being what they are, I picked three times as many as I ended up with but nevertheless, I got started from nothing using this highly efficient approach. You see, once I had identified those specific individuals, I did my research and sought out people who could make the introductions, which they gladly did. This was especially so with my contacts from professional organizations because I had devoted time to supporting their causes prior to asking my favors. I call this method top down because you start from the top! Bottoms up selling is just the opposite, whereby you do mass mailings hoping the right person will see it and be persuaded to call you. Bottoms up selling is inefficient, requires great patience, and at best achieves one and one half percent success. With top down selling, you get yourself introduced to the decision maker and make your presentation directly; the only other factor to consider is your closing ratio which for most savvy sales oriented small business owners can be as low as ten percent, but as high as fifty.

Keeping my top down selling approach in mind, review the following prospecting vehicles that can get you started:

- Newspapers (articles, ads, announcements that name new building sites, renovation projects, facilities managers, interior designers, etc.)
- Commercial interior design firms
- Informational seminars that you promote
- Professional organizations and their various functions
- (Volunteer for) board memberships
- Seminars that you attend
- Referrals
- Big ticket fund raiser dinners
- Church groups
- Private club memberships
- Large annual fund raiser golf tournaments
- Your CPA, corporate attorney, or business insurance agent
- Architectural firms
- Your stock broker
- Business consultants

The idea with all of the above is to immediately get into circles that will , in fact, put you no more than five people away from any one you wish to meet. One often-overlooked area that I have found it particularly easy to pursue is that of board memberships. At one point in my career, I positioned myself on a board that also had several presidents of medium sized firms. While I assure you I derived great satisfaction from working on the board's projects, the other benefit was the opportunity to get to know these decision-makers. One by one, I obtained permission to contact the vice-president or middle manager who was ostensibly in-charge, but in every case when I mentioned their president's name -- in the familiar!-- and that he/she had encouraged me to contact them, it was practically a done deal.

Another under-utilized prospecting vehicle is interior designers. It would make a world of sense to hand pick the commercial interior design firms you wish to make direct sales calls to and cultivate strong relationships. Let me describe one such meeting and its consequences.

First, the firm's production design director attended one of my free informational seminars that I conduct "advertising" my own art wholesaling business. I asked him if I could call the president of his firm directly and if he would pave the way. All went well and at my subsequent appointment with the president of this twenty-five year old commercial interior design firm. But surprisingly, I learned that I was the first art dealer to ever make a sales call with fine art packaged for volume sales. Needless to say, he happily agreed to meet with me further and provide me the opportunity to make my presentations on upcoming projects.

An important word about doing business through a third party such as an interior designer. Establish ahead of time that you will not contact the person's client without clearing it with them first and in all cases you will act as a sub-contractor unless otherwise stipulated. What this means in a nutshell, is that you will not try to steal their client out from under them. I can not tell you how much this will mean to these people. Reassurances in this area, along with your policies provided in writing (in your portfolio or brochure initially; contracts and letters of agreement later) can make it much easier for you to cultivate such relationships. By the way, the opposite is also true. If you go around breaking professional protocol and stealing other people's clients, you will not be nearly as successful as you certainly could. In fact, in so doing, your ethics, if not your intellect will become suspect.

Recording Your Communications

The same principals of documentation apply whether you are working on a sale to a final consumer or to a business. In order to properly service the client, you must retain key information about them. For example, when I sell art to small businesses, I will often make a preliminary site visit and record the following pertinent information as I do my "walk-through".

ART FOR BUSINESS
SITE SURVEY

Company
Name ______________________________Date________________

Contact
Name ______________________________Title________________

Decision
Maker(s)__________________________Co. Type____________

Address ________________________City __________State____

Zip___________ Phone______________ Fax________________

Page___________________Cellular_________________________

Additional Contact Persons:

Name ___________________________Position_______________

Phone__________________________

Name ___________________________Position_______________

Phone__________________________

Terms Agreed To:____

____

____

____

____

Description of Firm's Services/Products:______________________________
____
____

Target Market(s)____
____

Motto/Mission(s)____
____

Type of Visitors to Site & Impressions To Make ______________________
____
____
____

Select From Below Desired Impressions For Each Specific Area:

Animated	Lively	Bold	Cheerful	Energetic	Youthful
Serene	Gentle	Refined	Gracious	Tranquil	Soft
Classy	Vintage	Traditional	Antique	Thoughtful	Wise
Dynamic	Playful	Strong	Modern	Bright	Cutting Edge

Outside
Entrance ____________Lobby ____________Public_______________________

Exec.
Suites ______________Sales _____________Clerical _____________________

Conference Room(s)_____________Lunch Room _______ _____Hallways ___________________

Stated Art Style and Medium Preferences:

Abstract	Surrealism	Seascapes	Folk	Regional	Ethnic
Paintings	Prints	Sculpture	Posters	Landscapes	Photographic

Style Medium

Area____________________ ________________________________

Area____________________ ________________________________

Area____________________ ________________________________

Area____________________ ________________________________

Color Considerations (Obtain swatches)____________________________

Style Considerations (Obtain photos)______________________________

How Will Current Art Collection Be
Incorporated?____
____

Budget Range:

$1,000-$10,000 _______ $100,000-500,000 ________
$10,000-$25,000 _______ $500,000-$750,000 ________
$25,000-$100,000 _______ $750,000 or more ________

Timing Estimate:____

Funds Approved ______ Deposit Due______ Floor plan Obtained______

Installments Scheduled ________Artwork Selected __________________

Artwork Framed ______________Artwork Installed _________________

Final Inspection & Approval ________Final Installment ______________

Leasing (Optional) Paperwork Submitted For Approval________________

Now that you are ready (business plan, portfolio, and forms in-hand) you will begin the exciting adventure of prospecting. I define prospecting as the systematic sharing of valuable product or service information to a person capable of making a decision to buy in a reasonable time frame. This next section will assist you in that endeavor.

Sample Prospecting Scripts

As you review the following sample dialogues, remember you are top down selling, not cold calling. This implies you have done some research and have met the person in most instances (however briefly) prior to the first call. In some instances, you will have been given the person's name as a referral from someone you know. In either case, the opening will be much smoother compared to any attempt to cold call any businessperson. One thing you will notice in the "penetrating the receptionist" scenario -- I assume the art dealer, in this scenario, took the time to ask about the Executive Assistant in anticipation of forming a relationship. Believe me, if you intend to do much business with businesses, you need to develop the knack of building rapport with the "real person-in charge", as well as, the owner.

How To Best Work With The Receptionist/Secretary To Talk With Decision-Maker

The First Call:

Art Dealer: Hello, is John in?

Receptionist: May I tell him what this is concerning?

Art Dealer: Certainly. My name is Mary Jones. John and I chatted last week. He encouraged me to call and set up an appointment. Is this Susan McCrey, his Executive Assistant?

Receptionist: Yes, this is Susan. Mr. Baxter is out of the office (in a meeting or otherwise unavailable). Would you like to leave your number and I'll leave him your message?

Art Dealer: Great, although I'll be out and about so why don't I call back later. When would it be convenient to call back?

Receptionist: Mr. Baxter should be available tomorrow around 1:30 p.m.

Art Dealer: Thank you, Susan, I'll call back then. By the way, John has told me so much about you and the great job you are doing for him and the firm. I look forward to meeting you when I come in for my appointment with John. Well, I will call back tomorrow afternoon. Talk with you then.

<u>The Second Call:</u>

Art Dealer: Hello Susan. This is Mary Jones calling for John.

Receptionist: Oh hi, Mary. Please hold and I'll get him on the line. (Pause) Mr. Baxter is on another call; would you like to leave a message?

Art Dealer: Fine, Susan. By the way, do you know if he received my packet? It was in a large white envelope with photos of some office interiors enhanced with art. Great! Well, should I try after 3:00 p.m. or so today or would tomorrow be better?

Receptionist: He should be available later today.... oh, wait just a moment...he just finished his call. Let me put you through.

Once you get through to John, of course, simply sell the appointment. Do not get into a sales presentation about your art firm over the phone. This is something I learned a long time ago that helps me to stay focused. Always remember what you are selling at any given moment. Sometimes you are selling the idea of an introduction; other times it is the referral; in this instance it is the appointment. In fact, with most products and services it is quite easy to hold back by simply reminding the prospect that you will be sharing a highly visual experience (via your portfolio) at the appointment. You must first see the space that is to be adorned, then you will be able to recommend the artwork that will create the right "look" or alternatively, you must first "meet the people who are to be trained", etc.

I have included several examples for the greeting and qualifying steps in your initial appointment with the prospect for your careful review. For clarity, I have couched the examples in the art dealer scenario. Please keep in mind, (with some modifications) virtually the identical framework works whether you are selling consulting time, filters, art, or video training programs.

<u>At The Appointment--Greet Properly</u>

Art Dealer: Hello, John. Thank you, again for giving me an hour of your time today. I will do my best to make our time together as valuable as possible. (Brief Dialogue) Before we get started, how are the kids?

Hello, Mrs. Jones. I really appreciate the opportunity to meet today.

I'm truly excited about the possibility of working with you. Is an hour still good for you? Yes, Great. But before we started, how is the new house coming along? Won't it be completed soon? (Dialogue) N- Oh well, would you like to re-schedule or will thirty minutes be sufficient?

Well, it's so good to finally meet you in-person Mr. Baker. We have spoken so frequently on the phone, I feel we already know one another, don't you? (Response) Well, I know you are busy so why don't we verify the amount of time we can spend today on this project? (Response) Great - an hour is fine. Before we get started though, tell me about your golf tournament Saturday....

Hello Mr. McNamee. It is so good to meet you. My name again, is Martha Lance but feel free to call me Martha. (Dialogue) Great -- well, Tom it is for you then. Will an hour still work for you? (Response) Good. By the way, I want to compliment Mrs. Parker, your executive assistant -- she has been very helpful in giving me brochures about your firm so we could have a productive meeting today. (Dialogue)

The exact wording of your greeting is less important as long as you keep the following in mind:

• Always appear approachable and cheerful regardless of their demeanor.

• Open with what feels natural. When you are at an appointment you have already made one sale -- the appointment! So relax and make the most of the time allocated.

• Re-affirm with the client in the first three minutes the amount of time they have available. Then, make certain you pace yourself so you do not run out of time. In anticipation of last minute changes, always have a fifteen, thirty, forty-five and sixty minute presentation format each with their own appropriate opening, middle, and closing that you carefully choreograph.

• Shake hands, establish rapport and get on a first name basis (if you haven't already).

At The Appointment - Qualify Well

Art Dealer: What is your timing for this project?

Tell me again, what is your budget?

What artwork do you currently have in your corporate collection?

Were you looking for something that compliments your current collection or for a unique departure?

Can you give me an idea on what your expectations are for this art acquisition project?

Who have you done business with in the past?
(Response) What did you like most about them?
(Response) What would you like to see changed?
(Response)

Show me your current art collection. I would like to explore what it was about the art that inspired you to acquire it.

My firm has something to fit every budget. For those with unlimited resources, we have commissioned pieces

> and one of a kind originals by famous artists from $_______ to $_________. For those with moderate budgets, I can offer fine limited editions for only $________ to $___________. Plus, my firm has extensive offerings starting as low as $________ to $____________. What feels most comfortable for you?
>
> I sensed some urgency when we scheduled our meeting last week. Are you considering moving on this by the end of the week?
>
> Are you considering any other options or are you pretty well convinced we are the art sales firm for you?

The qualifying step for a top down selling approach depends on you completing some research prior to the first appointment. In fact, in many ways, you are simply re-qualifying because you would not have sold the appointment unless you had ascertained that a strong art acquisition possibility existed in the first place. Thus, you are only confirming that some discretionary dollars exist and that art acquisition is likely for the near future. You just want to know more specifically -- how much and when.

<u>Mail Follow-Up (Sample Letters)</u>

The following two letters are examples of what you might send after an initial discussion but prior to a formal appointment. The first letter assumes you had the opportunity to discuss your art firm in some detail with the prospect and/or the prospect comes as a very strong referral. The second letter assumes you have only met the prospect briefly. Review each one carefully and note the important differences in how you might wish to proceed.

Zella Jackson

Studio International

Mr. Robert Johnson, President January 5, 199X
Crescent Software Development Company
789 Rock Steady Way
Anytown, USA 96744

Dear Bob,

Thank you for the opportunity to talk with you about your firm's current and future art collection. It sounds like your software developers' enjoy environments that allow them to really think. As we discussed, art helps us to free up our minds. This, in turn, enhances both the quality and quantity of our work. My company, Studio International, is designed to help businesses who wish to enhance their interiors, improve productivity, strengthen morale and make a statement about the company's image.

I offer personalized consultations, creative custom framing and installation. My experienced staff will oversee each detailed step as the events of your project unfold, meeting your deadlines and ensuring you gratifying results.

Studio International's art selection includes original works, limited edition prints, paper sculpture, and monumental works from the finest contemporary artists in the world today. My consultations services are thorough and complete. I am confident I can provide you quality artwork and remain within the guidelines of your budget.

I am enclosing some full color brochures on two artists I felt you might like to explore further. When you mentioned you loved the classic impressionists and how, "classical artwork, like classical music helps us to tap into the creative genius we all have," -- I just had to share these artists with you. I will call you by the end of the week to set up an initial needs assessment meeting. I look forward to seeing you soon.

Warm regards,

Your Name

Studio International
123 Main Street • Anytown, USA 96744 • (800) 753-4337

Studio International

Mr. Thomas Jones,
Alternate Insurance Source
567 Shore Drive
Anytown, USA 96744

January 5,199X

Dear Mr. Jones,

It was a pleasure chatting with you at the Chamber of Commerce Mixer last week. Your business sounds like it has grown rapidly over the years.

Enclosed you will find a packet on Frederick Hart, the classical sculptor you were so intrigued with. As we discussed, his Vietnam War Memorial Sculpture is the most visited monument in the nation. I look forward to your firm becoming an important corporate collector of his work.

Thank you, in advance, for the opportunity to meet with you. I will call you by the end of the month to set up an appointment.

Regards,

Your Name

Studio International
123 Main Street • Anytown, USA 96744 (800) 753-4337

Your Sales Presentation

Your sales presentation to a business account will be similar to what you would present to a final consumer. Most books on selling will provide numerous examples of how to structure an effective sales presentation and I would encourage you to get one of the many such volumes on the market. Indeed, the broad subjects of marketing and selling require separate books, in and of themselves. For example, those in the art retailing business may elect to pick up two of my books entitled, The Art of Selling Art, and The Art of Creating Collectors which elaborate the fundamentals of selling and marketing for that particular industry.

The basics of developing an effective sales presentation, invariably revolve around sharing a well conceived, interactive presentation which details the facts and features of your product and/or service. When you are developing business accounts, however, there are some key points to keep in mind and will be explained in this section. Here again, I will stay with my art wholesaling scenario.

Preparation

You will first meet with the decision-maker and have determined the budget, time frames, and overall visual impressions desired. Then you will conduct a site survey and/or interview key personnel involved to fine tune desired impressions and match departmental level mottoes with the art in each area. Once this is completed, you will make a presentation to the owner who is sometimes alone, but in many cases is flanked by other key personnel. If the decision-maker is alone, then this presentation meeting will be as straightforward as it could possibly be. However, oftentimes, any additional personnel present can throat the art dealer who is seemingly put in the position of selling to a "committee". Experienced art dealers know this can be quite challenging. The best way to handle this is in the very beginning. When you have your initial meeting with the decision maker, always ask how any other key personnel (if at all) will enter into the decision making process (if at all). If the decision maker is unsure, then you will need to make an initial sale right there in the first appointment. You will sell the person on how the final presentation meeting will be handled, right down to getting permission to make an opening statement that reflects what the two of you agreed to. Here is one example agreement expressed as an opening statement:

> "Mr. Jones and I are delighted to have all of your input today, but as you know, managing by committee is an impossible task. So while each and every one of your opinions is important and will be taken into consideration, Mr. Jones has allowed me to be the tiebreaker based on his approval of my other art installation projects. Does that feel comfortable with every one?"

Having laid the groundwork, the balance of your preparation is straightforward enough although somewhat time consuming. Review the following checklist for important "homework" that should be completed prior to the big presentation.

- Portfolio or photo album with photos of past installations. Include letters of appreciation, "bullets" on your key services provided, and what sets you apart from the competition. Abbreviated biographies of the artists recommended for the project should also be included.
- Slides (or photos/slicks) of recommended artwork.
- A few carefully selected prints shrink-wrapped on foam core.
- One framed piece, ideally an original. If this proves impractical, you need a photograph of the framed original that will be the cornerstone of a key area or the entire collection.
- Sample moldings kit and swatches of matting options (materials and colors).

I realize the above checklist can take considerable time to put together. In my art wholesaling business, my staff designed and assembled all of the above for our network of art dealers. When you do it right, it does take time. On the other hand, as long as you have qualified the prospect properly-- know the budget and the timing -- then your time invested will pay-off royally. Lastly, never put all of your eggs in one basket. This is the one big mistake I have witnessed repeatedly. Art dealers will get one good lead and only pursue this one good lead. Invariably, all the time and effort to get such a sale seems wasted if no sale results. And yet, how many of us truly believe we posses a 100% closing ratio. If you really wish to pursue selling art to businesses, then anticipate your closing ratio and have enough projects percolating to assure a satisfactory level of success. Thus, all the time devoted will have a chance to pay-off and you will avoid getting discouraged.

Your Verbal Presentation

Now that your collateral material and props are in place, you will want to put some thought into your verbal presentation. Most of the steps apply have been expanded on in my earlier book, The Art of Selling Art. The nuances I wish to elaborate on now relate to satisfying the company's needs vs. the needs of any individual. Review the following examples and get some ideas.

> Frank Gallo has achieved texture and form in this cast paper sculpture. This supports your substance over style approach and becomes a visual expression of your firm's philosophy, doesn't it?
>
> This Frank Lisko graphic has a dynamic, bold feel. Wouldn't it enhance your sleek, modern interiors while supporting your "on the cutting-edge of technology" slogan?
>
> This abstract is dramatic style and conveys movement and action. Your ads say, "We move mountains for you!" Well, this Leung original painting appears to be a swirling mountain top in flight, and radiates your firm's mission with a passion, doesn't it?
>
> You mentioned you wanted to encourage a high-energy environment in your sales department. Well, this sweeping, colorful composition practically "leaps out from the canvas" and stimulates every viewer. Wouldn't this painting be the perfect focal piece for that department?
>
> I have taken the time to review research available on how colors affect morale and productivity levels in the work place. As you might imagine, mauves and pinks have a soothing, relaxing affect that can keep your software developers in a creative frame of mind. This painting is filled with those colors and has a place in your "think tank" area, doesn't it?

Similarly, the use of bolder more intense primary colors will stimulate an action response; as a result you will experience higher productivity. It is no coincidence that fast food restaurants make use of this research because they depend on their consumers eating and departing quickly during the peak lunch and dinner hours. Invariably, their color choices and decorative artwork displayed makes use of these kind of intense primary colors. Don't you feel that your deadline-driven word processing unit will benefit from the strong primary colors used in this abstract.

The areas where your staff members take their breaks should be tranquil yet rejuvenating. That is why I encourage you to put Diane Bartz's beautiful watercolors in these areas. Her landscapes depicting streams in forests are peaceful yet engage you with her curious play on colors... pink water, lilac leaves, and coral meadows... what a delight.

Seascapes and landscapes can be important for your staff members with no office windows. What a morale building way for management to say they care than with the addition of Lau Chun's flower-filled garden scenes.

Remember that the suggestions above hold true for firms that have a few departments and extend beyond the owner into a personality of its own. When you are dealing with a one-person show of a company then the guidelines for selling to a final consumer are more applicable. The tip-off revolves less around the actual size of the firm and more on what steps have already been taken to express the firm's persona -- in its stationary, logo, and advertising.

Now, I have fully explored with some detail using the "selling art to businesses" scenario. It was my hope to provide enough specifics so you could easily visualize the entire process of obtaining business accounts. As I mentioned earlier, if you modify the details, the same schema still applies to many products and/or services sold by home-based businesses to various small business target markets.

The Typical Life Cycle Of A Sale To Small to Medium-Sized Businesses

The typical sale to a business will take longer than one to a final consumer. The larger the firm and the potential sale, the lengthier its life cycle can become. A few months to a year before you close your first sale is not uncommon for what will become your larger accounts. Review the following to get a feel for all the steps in the typical first-time sale to a business.

• Prospect on a top-down basis; identify the business accounts you wish to make an initial appointment with.

• Determine who in your inner circle of influence can provide the referral or provide the introductions you desire, preferably with the owner, president, division head, etc. In your meeting with this ultimate decision-maker, verify how the final approvals will be handled in the event you land the project. If this is uncertain, come to a tentative, if not, definite agreement between the two of you as soon as possible. This is a separate and vital "sale", and you must close the person to avoid a great deal of wasted time and energy down the road.

• Always start at the top, even when you anticipate getting "kicked downstairs" because when the top person encourages you to speak to the "person in-charge", they will inevitably respond positively to your call. This will hold true as long as you give the person their "propers" and their son-in-law is not vying for the same project.

• Based on a referral or introduction, make your first phone call (and work effectively with the receptionist/secretary to get through to the decision-maker) to sell your first appointment.

• Schedule an initial needs assessment appointment whereby you qualify the project's timing and budget.

• If the timing is close enough in and budget sufficiently large, schedule your business site survey. As you walk the facility, re-affirm the project's timing and budget, attempt to expand the budget when client seems open, verify mottoes, creeds, productivity and morale objectives. Lastly, begin to make preliminary recommendations that seem to satisfy needs. This is done entirely in the descriptive. I save samples, swatches, etc. for my presentation.

• Send an invoice for the deposit you require. A twenty five percent deposit is reasonable on standard products; fifty percent for special orders. I also stipulate the payment schedule and terms in a contract that is subsequently signed by the delegated person in-charge. Depending on the complexity of the project you may wish to reverse the sequence of these events. However, I think you will find that for most projects up to $100,000 can be handled more simply. I send the invoice for the deposit before finalizing the contract because it helps the client to really think through what we have only talked about. If there are any hang-ups with the verbally shared budget, they will surface prior to the payment of any invoice. Thus, any major changes can be agreed to prior to putting all the paperwork together. I find this saves everyone a lot of time and energy. On projects exceeding $100,000, I will put the contract together prior to sending my first invoice. My concern with the larger projects has more to do with making sure the client is clear on major milestones, limits of liability, etc. These issues settled beforehand help protect yourself, as well as the client in the event problems arise.

• Give your first presentation. For larger projects whereby my presentation is to a group of two or more, I always hold back a bit because I anticipate having to respond to their reactions and come back at least one more time. I also recognize, the more complex the project, I may have to sequence my presentation into a series of several presentations whereby I have reserved some of my best for last to ensure a proper conclusion. This is why a typical sale to a business can get protracted. However, as long as you realize all of this ahead of time, you can enjoy the process rather than be perturbed by it.

• Once an overview schema has been decided upon, schedule follow-up appointments with only individuals as much as possible. This will facilitate the back end of the process and ensure deadlines are met. For example, if the department head of sales requires more time to make any final decisions on specific product or service selections (all choices will have been pre-approved at the group level), then do this just with that one person.

• Send out your invoices per the agreed upon schedule stipulated in the contract. One footnote here: many home- based business owners fail to have formal invoices printed with their company's logo, name, address, etc. Then they wonder why they are not paid in a timely fashion. Even worse, many small business owners will mail their hand-written invoice and get antsy after six days. Well, when you mail a hand-written invoice, invariably the accounts payable clerk will set it aside to check on it later because it doesn't look official which will cause delay. In addition, businesses almost always expect thirty days net (which means they will pay the invoice within 30 days of receipt) on all billings. Thus, under the best of circumstances, you will get your check mailed by the thirtieth day after you mailed your invoice. I mention this because for those of you whom this is news, nothing can ruin an otherwise great relationship faster than misunderstandings about money.

• Deliver the product and/or service. This could take several days or weeks depending on the complexity of the project. Once the project is completed, send your final invoice. Typically, the final ten-percent is not billed until your client has approved everything.

Once the project is completed, have professional photographs taken with your client's approval (or otherwise document the project) for inclusion in your portfolio. Now it is time to celebrate.

Leasing

Leasing is an attractive way for business accounts to acquire equipment. While I am neither an accountant or an attorney, and tax laws can change at a moment's notice, leasing products has proven advantageous for businesses and works very much like any other kind of lease that a company might have (auto, computer, etc.). These advantages include:

- Preserves your client's capital.
- Eases your client's cash flow.
- May offer client tax advantages.
- Allows client to have more product today (with minimal out-lay) thereby expanding the budget. In all cases, the leasing company will provide you the entire cash amount for the product upon delivery.

You can even have your clients "lease" your time. My husband sold custom software designed for small businesses for over ten years. He found a leasing company that would allow him to "bundle" his software, computer hardware (for which he was a rep), and his technical support time -- all in one. The leasing company was yet another small company like ours (a husband and wife team) who were accustomed and eager to work with our clientele.

There are firms that even specialize in leasing art such as LeaseArt in southern California, and there are those who wouldn't lease art if it were the last product on earth (I theorize this is due to the somewhat nebulas repossession/resale scenario for art as compared to commodity products such as cars). Your challenge is to find a leasing company that will work with your clients and make this option as straight forward as possible for them to get approved. Please note, however, if you are unsure about whether or not your client could qualify for a lease which could have stringent criteria, then do not recommend this option too early on. After all, if they ultimately qualify for a lease, it is much more desirable for you to have landed the project on a cash basis, gotten started, and subsequently reimburse the leasing company deposits then to recommend leasing early on and have the client not qualify thereby killing the project.

In summary, any woman who is dedicated to selling products and/or services to businesses can do so. And remember, when you create corporate accounts, you are creating wealth by providing valuable products and/or services to business owners who are very much like yourself.

Create A Business That Works For You

All too often, I consult with small to medium-sized business owners who feel their business is running them instead of the other way around. This is especially true of small retailers who may have leases that require the store to stay open seven days a week, including Christmas! I find myself working with such clients on how they should extract themselves from the business in an intelligent way. Oddly enough, the basis for this extraction often lies with reworking the company's basic foundation and redefining its marketing approach. I begin making my points with a true story, followed by guidelines that may well help you to create a business that works for you instead of the other way around.

One "Mom and Pop" Shop

I am reminded of a husband and wife team who had run a successful retail operation for over ten years. They retained me to overhaul their marketing program but were shocked when I asked to see their client files. All they had were the names and addresses of those who had merchandise shipped but NO phone numbers. In all of their decade of doing business, they had never thought to call a prior buyer and offer another buying opportunity. Because they were located in a tourist area, they felt it was simply improper to call clients (plus, I think there was a psychological barrier because most of their buyers lived thousands of miles away). These business owners were like most all around the country; while bright and articulate with an incredible talent for selecting merchandise and enormous stamina for "watching the shop," they were not reaching their sales potential due to erroneous attitudes about how to market effectively. I am proud to say that the couple in my story has implemented a client development program with its accompanying marketing program complete with periodic events, direct mail and phone follow-up promotions, and more - all done with flair. In the subsequent six years since I began working with them they have opened two new retail outlets and dramatically increased sales. Fully one-third of their sales are generated from repeat business. Needless to say, the amount of time "watching the shop" has diminished considerably and more time is spent having fun with their business and family. Moreover, they no longer "live and die" depending on traffic. What a relief!

I encourage you to make the very cornerstone of your business the development of loyal clientele. This holds true whether your business is retail, wholesale, home-based or otherwise. With this foundation in place, you can begin the methodical process of making it a real part of your daily business routines. To make the routine as effective as possible you must have many tools at your disposal. The rest of this section will provide you the framework from which to enjoy creating loyal, repeat buyers.

Higher Sales Plus Much More

Aside from the better sales you will achieve by cultivating strong repeat buyers, there are perhaps more fundamental reasons to pursue this approach to business. The realities of today's marketplace tell us consumers and business buyers alike want, if not demand, personalized and convenient service. Today, the share of consumer and business purchases transacted by telephone, mail order, and cable TV is growing at an unprecedented rate. Financial institutions have made remote shopping simple through the use of bankcards, giving the consumer the bonus of improved record keeping as a free spin off.

In addition, prosperous Americans are busy people who wish to simplify their lives. They long for personalized service from business people they trust and with whom they have a long-standing relationship. When you stop and think about it, these relationships express the very best of humankind: people who appreciate the hard work and high quality services provided by another human being much like themselves. Moreover, you and the buyer appreciate, respect, trust, and enjoy your mutually satisfying relationship. What a great way to live.

So, as I speak about record keeping, direct mail design, planning, organizational tools and the like, please keep in mind that these are only devices which assist you in your endeavors. It will be your "win-win" attitude that will imbue your every sales presentation, letter, and event invitation with exciting energy required to take you to your top. On the other hand, if you really don't want to know how the important details of your client's home, office, or business -- no amount of record keeping or planning will sustain your firm. Only your heartfelt connection with your clients as human beings will inspire you and them toward visionary outcomes. What would it be like to have most of your buyers who began with a $500 acquisition and evolve to acquire thousands of dollars worth of your merchandise? Similarly, what would it feel like to have a new client contract for an initial $1,000 worth of your time and later develop them into a loyal retainer client investing $20,000 per year with you? Finally, what impact would it have on your firm if those buyers who <u>started</u> with a $25,000 equipment order -- all <u>ended</u> with that million dollar collection? With the philosophical framework described below, coupled with your "win-win" attitude, you will begin the lifelong odyssey of creating loyal clientele.

THE FACTS

By developing your own customized client development program and planning a comprehensive marketing program complete with events, direct mail/phone campaigns, etc., you can accomplish the following:

1. EXPAND YOUR MARKET: By establishing solid relationships with all of your high-end prior buyers, they will reciprocate with your encouragement, to provide you qualified referrals. In fact, studies indicate a satisfied client will provide an average of five qualified referrals. Some will give you zero while others will give you everyone out of their organizer! Thus, a systematic way to obtain referrals should be part of your marketing program.

2. OBTAIN REPEAT BUSINESS: A previous buyer is six times more likely to buy from you than "cold" traffic. Therefore, one-third or more of your advertising and promotional dollars should be earmarked for obtaining repeat business.

3. IMPROVE CLIENT SATISFACTION: The market of the '90s and beyond demand high quality, personalized service. Once you provide this, the likelihood of obtaining referrals and repeat sales goes up.

4. CULTIVATE CLIENT LOYALTY: I am sure you recognize from numerous psychological profile studies that fully 60% to 65% of the population are deliberative thinkers and loyalists. Thus, we can faithfully construct promotions in a routine fashion that in fact, routinizes the purchases of the majority of your buyers...who enjoy said routine!

5. EXEMPLIFY PROFESSIONAL SELLING STANDARDS: As we strive to make our business successful, I trust you wish to be professional about your dealings. When you follow a client development program you tell your buying world that you stand behind your product/service, respect each individual, and follow through on commitments in an orderly, proactive manner. All things being equal, when a client is given a choice they will most certainly place their loyalties with the professionally run firm rather than the unprofessional one.

Your Client Development Program

Stephen Covey, national best selling author (The Seven Habits of Highly Effective People, among others) popularized the notion, "begin with the end in mind." By starting with this simple thought, you can flesh out the details of your own customized client development program.

For example, what does the typical small business owner say to a prospect at a trade show? More often than not, you hear, "Well, Madame (or sir), now that you have seen our product line, would you mind signing our guest book?" After four days of this, what do you end up with? A very long list of "maybes".... if you are lucky. If you are unlucky, you will end up with a very long list of "polite, postponed no's!"

In contrast, I ask the following at trade shows, "Well, Mr. Jones, you mentioned this would be a good time to consider that installation. Would I be able to provide you a firm quote by the end of next week? (Pause for response) Great, because I feel confident when you compare us to our competition, we will always save you time and money while providing superior service. In fact, Mr. Jones, I view this as a starting point for a lifelong mutually beneficial relationship." What do you think the majority of Mr. Jones' will say to this?. After four days of this line of questioning at that same trade show, you will end up with a short but very sweet list of strong "maybes", plus some definite "yeses".

In short, you begin selling the potential client on the very notion of a lengthy, if not lifelong relationship before you ever create a transaction. My clients who have been on my customized client development programs for many years tell me it has added upwards of thirty percent additional gross revenue each year as well as the reward of knowing you have earned the trust and loyalty of respected members of your community.

Realize Financial Independence Through Your Firm's Profits

When you create a business that works for you, it will also provide the additional revenue you are planning for to realize financial independence. This is the stuff American Dreams are made of. First, it is perfectly legal for you to expense the majority of your expenditures right out of your business. This minimizes your tax obligations while maximizing your income stream. This is particular valuable for those who already have a mortgage and do not anticipate moving for several years because you no longer need to "qualify" for the most house you can afford. Once you are in a home mortgage, you can work to minimize your taxes (through small business ownership) which in affect increases your income.

For example, the same expense allowances are available to the small home-based business owner as the owner of a chain of retail stores or a large manufacturing business: company cars, computers, pens, paper and pencils, television sets, VCR's, child care, car, liability, health and life insurance, travel expenses, gasoline, even entertainment expenses . Since tax laws vary from state to state and can change at a moment's notice, I rely (as I recommend you do) on a tax accountant to "bless" my tax returns. However, the reality is that essentially every conceivable expenditure that is construed to be business related can be deducted from your gross revenues leaving minimal net taxable revenues. Consequently, you will enjoy a higher standard of living with the opportunity to invest much larger sums of money than previously possible as an employee.

Chapter IX
Woman, Take Charge!

We Can Do It!

I believe this baby is a queen,
there's something about the song she sings...
-- she'll reign supreme.

I believe this child is a star,
there's something about her words; they've wings!
-- She will go far.

I believe this woman will achieve,
there's something about her dreams -- we are
-- what we believe.

Z.J. 1983

Do "grand" personalities shape the world? I don't think so. When all is said and done, “sheroes” are everyday people -- people like you and me, who take the time to make a difference in someone else's life.

Let's Take Back Our Nation

Together, we can change the world. And change it we must. If we collectively take up the sword of economic power in this country, we will begin to influence our legislators where it counts -- in their pocketbooks. We can begin the slow process of reclaiming this country and putting it squarely back in the hands of enterprising citizens and less in the control of small but powerful special interest groups. This small business movement needs your support for a cause so mighty no enterprising citizen can possibly ignore it.

This country was founded on the principles of rugged individualism with little government involvement in our lives and businesses. Somewhere along the way we lost that vision and have become a nation with 26% of its population on the public doles. It does not take a genius to figure out that if we continue in this direction, soon there will simply not be enough taxpayers to pay the enormous "bills" from our socialistic programs. What this country needs are more enterprising citizens who are self-employed or owners of small businesses who will contribute to society in a productive way. This will serve to strengthen our economy on the one hand and enhance individuals' sense of self-worth on the other.

One of the first things I'll implore you to do once you have established your small business is to write or fax your congressperson and tell him/her to lessen the paperwork and tax burden on the small business owner. Tell the person how much you pay yourself and tell them to reduce their salaries for the sake of the nation. As ludicrous as this may sound, such a grassroots appeal could begin the avalanche that is needed to get important changes in place that will allow the small business owner to work less encumbered by government while providing the impetus for a healthier, stronger economy.

The National Federation of Independent Business (NFIB) is an organization you may wish to join and support. In 1996 it represented 600,000 small businesses. NFIB members employ more than seven million people and report annual gross sales of nearly $750 billion. Their typical member employs five to six people, makes $42,000 a year, and averages about $250,000 to $300,000 in annual income.

Jack Faris, President of the NFIB made the following observations in the June, 1996 IMPRIMIS Newsletter.

"It doesn't matter if business owners are men or women, whites, blacks, or Hispanics, southerners, northerners,, easterners, or westerners, manufacturers or services providers. They all agree that the greatest obstacle to success in America today is big government.

If the business of America were politics, we would be in deep trouble. But it is not. The business of America is *small business*. Half of all Americans live in small business households. But the people who have a stake in the future of small business are not just those who are owners, managers, or employees. They are the people who know that:

- The name of the game today is not pork; it is potential. It is the potential for new businesses, new jobs, and new services.

- This is a pivotal time in our nation's history, a time to make decisions not just about a balanced budget but about the fundamental nature of government.

- And, most important of all, no matter how busy we are, we must get involved in solving the problems of our society."

Diana Furchgott-Roth and Christine Stolba are the authors of the report entitled, "Women's Figures". They paint a promising economic present and future for enterprising women with statistics like, "women aged 27 to 33 who had never had a child earned 98 percent of men's wages." These statistics fall short when the real world suggests that successful women should not have to forgo childbearing in order to earn on par with men. In addition, syndicated columnist, Mona Charen observed after reading "Women's Figures" that, "The story of women's economic success in the past quarter century has been breathtaking. But the effects of such a huge social movement have not been all positive. When women left homemaking, they also left neighborhood-making, and school-making, and morality enforcing, We haven't yet figured out how to fill the gap they left behind."

American women have a legacy for starting important grassroots campaigns that over time have made sweeping changes in this country's laws and society. For women of the baby boom era, let us not forget that it was our grandmothers who fought and won our right to vote and provided the impetus for ***legal*** birth control. Granddaughters of America, I appeal to you now to leave a legacy that is no less important to your own grandchildren; one that provides them a healthier business climate and a greater chance at becoming successful entrepreneurs. Since the single fastest growing segment in the private sector is female business owners, it becomes imperative that we join the ranks of those involved in protecting our freedom to enterprise.

Take Charge of Your Life

To take charge of your life, you must first know, understand, and love this unique person that you are. It is to know what you feel and to speak those truths. It is to believe what you feel is vitally important to share. And to share -- you must, even if you risk offending some people along the way. Because you are so convinced of your "call to action" that you spare nothing in you to convey your message. Indeed, it means making the choice to have a message. It means no less than living your life with purpose.

As I journeyed through life I discovered there were many women who would not allow themselves certain basic freedoms. The freedom to work on issues, with people, and in working environments that allowed them to be themselves. I have literally met thousands of women through my seminars and over the phone that are in the process of "fixing" themselves. The laments may sound familiar:

> "Don't tell anyone but....
>
> I grew up poor so I need to work hard.
>
> Or...
>
> I grew up with an alcoholic father so I need to work hard and prove myself to the world.
>
> Or...
>
> I grew up well-to-do but my parents never had time for me so I am depressed.
>
> Or...
>
> I was adopted and never forgave my mom for giving me away.
>
> Or...
>
> Oh, and don't tell anyone because I am ashamed."

My favorite of all is, "I grew up well-to-do, my parents had plenty of time for me and I still don't know what to do with myself". Well, for you, I say look around -- there's a neighbor who needs your help.

The laments are endless but they all say the same thing. I need to get "fixed", then I will be acceptable..... accepted. Oh, but herein lies the rub. There is nothing wrong with you. There is nothing to fix. And you do not need to be accepted. You are who you are. Those experiences that you may feel ashamed of have created your own rich tapestry of emotions; your own unique character. They, in turn, can provide you the foundation for your message; the backdrop for your purpose; the heart and soul of your business.

If you grew up poor, go ahead and work hard; but share your experiences and be an inspiration to other impoverished young people. If you grew up with an alcoholic parent, rejoice because you have learned valuable lessons about addiction. Share them and help others live a better life.

If your parents neglected you because they themselves were too busy working for "things", set yourself free by sharing those experiences with other workaholics so they won't make the same mistake.

If your birth mom felt she had to let you go -- celebrate because you know the profound wisdom that goes along with being abandoned. Share your experiences with other adoptees or perhaps with a pregnant teenager so she may make the best choice.

The message you have inside you is waiting to come out. Share it. You see, if you live with purpose, then you will automatically create a visionary plan for yourself and in the process take charge of your life.

Luckily, I discovered ME. I learned to dismiss the idea of being broken and the need to be fixed and accepted. And in the process I found freedom. Freedom to be a woman, a person of color, a human being who writes business books and poetry, lectures all over the country, collects art and jewelry, plays the piano, nurtures my children, cries, wears braces, laughs, and most of the time... be happy.

So, if you are looking for the key to take charge of your life. Look no further than the mirror. <u>You</u> have been here all along.

Take Charge of Your Business

Now that you have started your business, muster all the passion, resolve, and perseverance you can because you are going to need it. Keep your eyes and ears on the vision and the short-term hurdles will seem less formidable. Make certain that everyone who you rely on -- spouse, staff members, suppliers, and sub-contractors are, in fact, reliable for the key pulse points of your day-to-day business life. And when your spouse needs a break, give him that space.

Put the past out back, your vision out front, and keep your passion burning brightly inside. If you get a "no" when you need a "yes", move on to the next resource. There is no reason to "buy in" to someone else's negativity. Remember that you create your world through your own unique vision and hopefully those around you whom you depend on align their visions (at least temporarily) with yours.

Take Charge of Your Neighborhoods, Families, & Homes

If the men of this country are (statistically) less involved– then the women of this country ***must*** be. Take the time to be part of your local schools, neighborhood boards, and act as the leader of your family that you need to be. What greater power can we wield than the power of influence over the next generations?

Once you place your community in your top priorities and position it appropriately in your long-term written plan, you are on your way to becoming a community leader. And it doesn't take much. Once you make the decision and get connected with the key pulse points of your community, the organizations you become involved in will take care of the rest. Your PTA, local sports organizations, churches, charity boards, professional organizations, etc. all need and want your help. Moreover, your children will be inspired by your participation. In so doing, you will find yourself a role model and helping to develop the next generation of involved citizens.

If your husband is on the traditional path to success, he may well have little time to assist with the children after school. Homework, serious hobbies/lessons, sports, etc. require a parent to be involved. And when the stress of over-extended lifestyles is eliminated from your life, these can be some of the most rewarding times you will spend with your children. Even if your children are not that active outside the home, your presence, supervision, and availability are vital for their healthy development.

Let Yourself Grow

Perhaps the greatest gift you can give yourself is the opportunity to grow and change. The healing power of moving on to higher ground is the best medicine available for optimal mental health.

My first lesson on this important issue came when I was a department manager at IBM. I had the pleasure of having a truly outstanding woman on my team... Beth Olson.

Beth had been with the company for over forty five years; almost twenty years longer than I had been on the this earth. Beth was about to retire in a few weeks and I asked her a rather personal question. I said, "Was it right, those forty five plus years here?" She told me, "It was right at the time, but do you know what I really want to do now? -- I want to dance, professionally!"

I did not laugh, as I am sure others might. I found that this woman had been an avid ballroom dancer for nearly two decades. She and her husband danced three times a week without fail. Not only did they dance, they played tennis, swam, -- both possessed superior physical vitality. I subsequently had a chance to see Beth and her husband dancing; they were poetry in motion.

I shared, "Beth, go for it; do it! Then, I witnessed the same awakening in her that I had seen on the faces of the young people I had lectured to.

Why, this worldly and experienced gentlewoman was still searching. And I don't mean that negatively, not at all! She was growing, evolving, and flexing her dream muscles. I thought, how fantastic. I discovered that perhaps in the final analysis, the answer to the question, "Do you know where you are going?", can not be described in terms of a destination. Because when you are experiencing true personal growth, there is no final destination. There is only the journey, itself.

Give Our Children The Brightest Melody For Their Journey

We must take on a campaign to change the attitudes of American men and women and we must do this primarily through our actions, which speak of self-sufficiency and independence. We must help the teachers of our children to view boys and girls equal in talent and comparable in their ability to fully participate in business even though girls may, in many instances, go on a decidedly different course. We must help our children see that when one group in our society receives unfair treatment, the entire society suffers degradation.

I believe the challenges and confrontations presented by the business world can only be resolved through awareness, astute life planning, entrepreneurial pursuits, and an absolute commitment to success.

All too often, women never learn to dance without a partner. Building a successful business can mean monetary security and independence -- dignity. It can mean the difference between truly sharing your life with the man of your dreams and simply putting your life in his hands.

Small children by virtue of their youth and inexperience, do not "know" that genitals limit aspirations. We must teach our daughters to continue to listen to the music they heard as small children so that they might choose to pick up their feet and dance.

As we move forward to create our story -- herstory -- I am filled with hope and anticipation for our own granddaughters. In the year 2070 - ***just one lifetime from now*** - perhaps our granddaughters will be able to say with confidence:

> "Our lives resonate with the true rhythms of womanhood. We are free to enterprise and create wealth, ...to conceive and bear children.... to devote time to our loved ones as well as devote time to ourselves. We are truly free!"

Chapter X.
Epilogue

"WHAT LIES BEHIND US AND WHAT LIES BEFORE US ARE TINY MATTERS COMPARED TO WHAT LIES WITHIN US."

Oliver Wendell Holmes

Those of us fortunate enough to ponder purpose must first be thankful to have had such rich, fulfilling lives that we have the time to ponder such imponderables. Indeed, as I reflect over my challenging yet rewarding journey, I – for one, am profoundly grateful to have lived a life of purpose. When did I find my purpose? Oh, that may be trying to put too fine a point on it. What I do know is this:

Women who choose to enterprise need to know they have viable choices that can mean a balanced life through entrepreneurship that leaves ample time for children, spouses, friendships, neighbors, schools, hobbies – well, for living. This kind of life can be accomplished with the right preparation, planning, and choices. Often these choices depart dramatically from the traditional male patterns of success.

It took me a lifetime to come to grips with defining my life on my own terms; a life filled with purpose, family, and balance. I am rewarded to find my experiences can illuminate the lives of others that needn't reinvent this wheel. It is time for me to step up to the podium and share even more.

My purpose is in concert with the rest of the nation as millions flock to the nest as home-based business owners. I have worked to provide guidelines in this book to assist those seeking not just a busy life but one that provides financial independence and self-sufficiency while leaving ample time for children, friends, spouses, and hobbies.... a life that flows with the rhythms of womanhood.

When I look back over my life as an educator, leader, coach, and counselor... perhaps I really began to get in touch with my purpose when I was barely fifteen years old. My baby sister was three and a willing student. Since we were poor, I made books from blank sheets of paper and taught my young preschooler to read and "figure" before she could speak clearly. The look of discovery in her eyes forever awakened in me the desire to teach.

Those first glimpses of purpose became muddled as misguided teachers showed me the wrong paths. Corporate America, nine-to-five, Dilbert and company proved hostile to female bio-forms; not by plan but by their very nature. My meteoric rise at IBM proved to me that I could do "it" but the question remained, "why?"

But the "why" of life is never more profound that when asked at its end. My baby sister and I said goodbye for the last time nearly three years ago when she succumbed to breast cancer. She had lived a life of co-dependency, poverty, and single-parenthood. How had I made such a difference in so many others' lives, but not hers? Imponderable! We each have our own lives to live and clearly, making the right choices remains an individual's responsibility. But was her death, in part, a warning for me to get on with it? She always said that I was a great teacher.

When did I find my purpose? Oh Life! You are such a finely woven tapestry that makes the answer to that question yet another imponderable. Where did I find my purpose? That I know as precisely as I know my own name because my journey to purpose put me on a sandy, white beach in the afternoon of my life.

I set myself free on Maui in the shadow of Mt. Haleakala. There like no place on earth, the mountain rises 10,000 feet skyward and the ocean spills 12,000,000 feet seaward toward a continent half way 'round the world. It was there in Wailea, Maui, where I first allowed "me to be."

I listened to the ocean pulsate for nearly a thousand nights. The rhythmic waves made a new music and I imagined a New World. While the nights were awash in blackness, the answers shined brighter than a mid-day tropical sun. I, the great, great granddaughter of a slave woman finally allowed myself to be free!

Someone wise once said, "While you may never know where you were lost, you can never forget where you were found." On a wide, sandy white beach in the middle of nowhere but at the heart of it all, I found myself. I am confident the wisdom I have gained was placed in my heart as a willing teacher to educate others to find their way.

I alluded throughout this volume that my purpose for sharing was to assist other enterprising women in their quest for a better life – but there is another reason. It is to honor my baby sister who died never knowing the right paths from which to choose. I honor her with my life's work because she was *the student* who awakened *the teacher* in me.

About the Author

Zella Jackson has been an independent Business Development Consultant since 1981. She is an expert marketing and sales professional and has developed an international reputation in the fine art industry.

As a recognized expert, she has been a featured speaker at major Art Expos and Art Dealer Conventions such as **Art Expo New York**, **Arte'**, and **Hawaii Art Expo**, and the biannual Mill Pond Press Dealer Convention. Art Expo New York annually attracts over 100,000 visitors each year and is considered the largest of its kind in the world today. Also, art trade journals such as **Decor Magazine**, **Preview Magazine**, **Art Trends**, **Art Expressions** and **Art Business News** have published her articles on such topics as "Creating Advertising That Works", "The Art of Selling Art", and "Art Buying Trends". She does a syndicated column for the internationally distributed publication, **Art Expressions**. In addition, she has been featured on nationally syndicated radio talk shows like ***CNN's radio affiliate*** (syndicated in over 300 cities nationwide) to talk about "The Art of Collecting Art".

Nationally known author, lecturer and guest speaker featured in educational films and publications. She wrote "**The Art of Selling Art**", first released in 1988. The revised 1994 edition was released in the fall of that year along with her companion books, **"The Art of Creating Collectors"** and **"The Gallery Management Manual"**. In addition, she is the principal researcher and co-author of a coffee table book entitled, **"Artists of Hawaii",** was released November 1994.

Zella has taught collegiate level classes at Hawaii Pacific University and San Francisco City College. In addition, she has been called as an expert witness in court trials.

Zella's community involvement spans twenty-five years beginning with her freshman year in college. She speaks often at local schools, universities, and conferences concerning Entrepreneurism, African American History, Financial Independence for Women, and Small Business Development. She has served on the boards of YMCA, Northern California Black Engineering Society, Hawaii Federation of Business and Professional Women, United Way, Parent Participation Nursery School, MESA (Math, Engineering, and Science Achievement), among others. She is currently a member of Central Valley's Mother of Twins Club and is active in organizing their 31st Annual, 1998

MOTS California State Convention. It is projected to draw members from all over the state.

Zella has a BS degree in Mechanical Engineering and an MBA in Operations Management from Michigan State University. Formerly, IBM's General Products Division Systems Operations Manager with multi-million dollar budget responsibility. As a former Marketing Specialist for Dow Chemical Company, she headed a successful national marketing campaign.

Selected in 1992 as a Who's Who Among Rising Young Americans. Was also awarded the State of Hawaii Career Woman of the Year Award in 1982.

Zella's hobbies include biking, reading, traveling, and piano playing. She has trained for several bike marathons including centuries (100 miles in one day). After spending fifteen years in the Hawaiian Islands, she is currently living in the beautiful Sierra foothills with her three children and husband of twenty years.

"I'D RATHER HAVE MY HANDS FULL THAN EMPTY."

Mother of triplets

Pamela Patrick Novotny
Joy of Twins

To Order Additional Copies of this Book

Send Postal Orders to: Novasearch Publishing
29643 Horseshoe Drive
Coarsegold, CA 93614

Or Call to Order: (209) 642-6181

Shipping: First Class $3.00 per book

Please mail book(s) to:

Name: ______________________________

Street: ______________________________

City ______________________________

State ______________________________

Zip ______________________________

			# of copies		
Price:	$19.95	X	_______	=	________
Shipping:	$ 3.00	X	_______	=	________
Total:					________

Please make checks payable to **Novasearch Publishing**

Visa, Master Card and American Express accepted

Card Number: _______________ ***Expiration:*** _____

Name on Card: ______________________________